Harvard Business Review

ON

FINDING AND KEEPING

THE BEST PEOPLE

THE HARVARD BUSINESS REVIEW PAPERBACK SERIES

The series is designed to bring today's managers and professionals the fundamental information they need to stay competitive in a fast-moving world. From the preeminent thinkers whose work has defined an entire field to the rising stars who will redefine the way we think about business, here are the leading minds and landmark ideas that have established the *Harvard Business Review* as required reading for ambitious businesspeople in organizations around the globe.

Other books in the series:

Harvard Business Review Interviews with CEOs

Harvard Business Review on Brand Management

Harvard Business Review on Breakthrough Thinking

Harvard Business Review on Business and the Environment

Harvard Business Review on the Business Value of IT

Harvard Business Review on Change

Harvard Business Review on Corporate Governance

Harvard Business Review on Corporate Strategy

Harvard Business Review on Crisis Management

Harvard Business Review on Decision Making

Harvard Business Review on Effective Communication

Harvard Business Review on Entrepreneurship

Harvard Business Review on Knowledge Management

Harvard Business Review on Leadership

Harvard Business Review on Managing High-Tech Industries

Harvard Business Review on Managing People

Harvard Business Review on Managing Uncertainty

Harvard Business Review on Managing the Value Chain

Other books in the series (continued):

Harvard Business Review on Measuring Corporate Performance
Harvard Business Review on Mergers and Acquisitions
Harvard Business Review on Negotiation and Conflict Resolution
Harvard Business Review on Nonprofits
Harvard Business Review on Strategies for Growth
Harvard Business Review on Work and Life Balance

Harvard Business Review

ON

FINDING AND KEEPING THE BEST PEOPLE

The *Harvard Business Review* articles in this collection are available as individual reprints. Discounts apply to quantity purchases. For information and ordering please contact Customer Service, Harvard Business School Publishing, Boston, MA 02163. Telephone: (617) 783-7500 or (800) 988-0886, 8 A.M. to 6 P.M. Eastern Time, Monday through Friday. Fax: (617) 783-7555, 24 hours a day. E-mail: custserv@hbsp.harvard.edu

Library of Congress Cataloging-in-Publication Data
Harvard business review on finding and keeping the best people.
        p.   cm. — (Harvard business review paperback series)
    Includes index.
    ISBN 1-57851-556-4 (alk. paper)
    1. Employees—Recruiting.   2. Employee retention.   I. Title: On finding and keeping the best people.   II. Title: Finding and keeping the best people.   III. Harvard business review.   IV. Series.
HF5549.5.R44 H287   2001
658.3´111—dc21   00-052987
                                                              CIP

The paper used in this publication meets the requirements of the American National Standard for Permanence of Paper for Publications and Documents in Libraries and Archives Z39.48-1992.

Contents

Harvard Business Review

ON

FINDING AND KEEPING
THE BEST PEOPLE

Toward a Career-Resilient Workforce

ROBERT H. WATERMAN, JR., JUDITH A.
WATERMAN, AND BETSY A. COLLARD

Executive Summary

VIRTUALLY EVERYONE AGREES that the old covenant between employer and employee—under which companies offered at least a measure of job security in exchange for adequate performance and some exhibition of loyalty—is dead. Some management thinkers argue that instead of the traditional focus on *employment,* the focus should now be on *employability.* That means having the competitive skills required to find work, when you need it, wherever you can find it. But that notion does not spell out what responsibilities companies now have to employees and vice versa.

In this article, the authors say the answer is a new covenant under which the employee and the employer share responsibility for maintaining—even enhancing—the individual's employability both inside *and outside* the company. It is the company's responsibility to provide

1

employees with the tools, the open environment, and the opportunities for assessing and developing their skills. It is the employee's responsibility to manage his or her own career and to show some commitment to the company's purpose and community for as long as he or she works there. The result is a group of self-reliant workers—or a *career-resilient* workforce—and a company that can thrive in an era in which the skills needed to remain competitive are constantly changing.

Some companies, such as Apple Computer, Sun Microsystems, Raychem, and 3Com, are already moving in this direction. And from their progress so far, the authors can discern basic ingredients all programs should include and pitfalls to avoid.

The company that embraces career resilience will have a huge strategic advantage. By encouraging people to grow, to change, and to learn, it will do those things better itself.

P EOPLE MOURN ITS PASSING: the longtime covenant between employee and employer. We remember fondly the days when IBM could offer lifetime employment. And even if we didn't work for the likes of IBM, most of us understood that respectable companies would offer at least a measure of job security in exchange for adequate performance and some exhibition of loyalty. No longer. While a few prominent companies argue that the old covenant still exists, most people—and most companies—now hardened by downsizings, delayerings, right-sizings, layoffs, and restructurings, have concluded that the old covenant is null.

But what will take its place? Some management thinkers are arguing that instead of the traditional focus on *employment,* the focus should now be on *employability.* In other words, we should forget about clinging desperately to one job, one company, or one career path. What matters now is having the competitive skills required to find work when we need it, wherever we can find it.

Is that it? A workforce of loners roaming corporate halls, factories, and E-mail systems? What responsibility, if any, does a company now have to employees? Ought management be concerned only about staying lean to keep up with competition and not about acting mean? Should management be satisfied with employees whose only loyalty is to their own careers? How can an enterprise build capabilities, forge empowered teams, develop a deep understanding of its customers, and—most important—create a sense of community or common purpose unless it has a relationship with its employees based on mutual trust and caring? And how can an enterprise build such a relationship unless it commits something to employees and employees commit something to it?

The answer is by entering into a new covenant under which the employer and the employee share responsibility for maintaining—even enhancing—the individual's employability inside *and outside* the company. Under the old covenant, employees entrusted major decisions affecting their careers to a parental organization. Often, the result was a dependent employee and a relatively static workforce with a set of static skills. Under the new

Self-reliant workers stand ready to reinvent themselves in order to keep pace with change.

covenant, employers give individuals the opportunity to develop greatly enhanced employability in exchange for better productivity and some degree of commitment to company purpose and community for as long as the employee works there. It is the employee's responsibility to manage his or her own career. It is the company's responsibility to provide employees with the tools, the open environment, and the opportunities for assessing and developing their skills. And it is the responsibility of managers at all levels to show that they care about their employees whether or not they stay with the company. The result is a group of self-reliant workers—or a *career-resilient workforce*—and a company that can thrive in an era in which the skills needed to remain competitive are changing at a dizzying pace.

By a career-resilient workforce, we mean a group of employees who not only are dedicated to the idea of continuous learning but also stand ready to reinvent themselves to keep pace with change; who take responsibility for their own career management; and, last but not least, who are committed to the company's success. For each individual, this means staying knowledgeable about market trends and understanding the skills and behaviors the company will need down the road. It means being aware of one's own skills—of one's strengths and weaknesses—and having a plan for enhancing one's performance and long-term employability. It means having the willingness and ability to respond quickly and flexibly to changing business needs. And it means moving on when a win-win relationship is no longer possible.

A workforce that is constantly benchmarking and updating its skills is one that not only responds to change but anticipates it. Competitiveness—keeping close to customers, staying on top of technology and market trends, and striving to be ever more flexible—becomes everyone's responsibility, not that of just a handful of executives. All employees become involved in shaping the company's strategy, in shifting the company's collective eyes from navels to market forces. By looking out for themselves, employees look out for the company.

Sound far-fetched? Some companies are already moving in this direction. Not surprisingly, many of them are located in Silicon Valley, where the struggle to cope with the ever-faster pace of change has long been a way of life. These pioneers include Apple Computer; Sun Microsystems, the workstation manufacturer; Raychem Corporation, a manufacturer of specialized industrial products; and 3Com Corporation, a maker of computer-networking products. These companies are in various stages of implementing programs to create a career-resilient workforce. While their approaches may differ, they share a common aim: to give employees the power to assess, hone, redirect, and expand their skills so that they stay competitive in the job market. In return, they expect employees to make a bigger contribution to the company. "Companies must shift from using and then harvesting employees to constantly renewing employees," says Robert J. Saldich, president and CEO of Raychem and an ardent proponent of the new covenant.

This approach requires a sea change in attitudes and values. First, the traditional definition of loyalty must go. Companies can no longer take the view that talented employees who jump ship are betraying them. Nor can individuals take the view that they've been betrayed when a company no longer needs their skills. On the other hand, employees must feel like valued, trusted, and respected members of the corporate community while they are a part of it.

Second, the usual view of a career path must change. In the old days, it pretty much meant sticking with one company and rising in one specialty area. These days, both companies and employees are healthier if employees have multiple skills, if they can move easily across functional boundaries, if they are comfortable switching

The traditional parent-child relationship between employer and employee must give way to an adult-adult relationship.

back and forth between regular duties and special projects, and if they feel comfortable moving on when the right fit within one company can no longer be found.

Third, all employees—not just bosses—must be much more aware that the purpose of the organization is to provide goods and services that customers value, and that if the organization does not do that, nobody in it will have a job. The corollary is that the organization has room only for people who contribute to creating such goods and services.

Fourth, a new relationship must be established between the organization and its employees. The traditional parent-child relationship must give way to an adult-adult relationship, and this applies to the organization's way of dealing with all employees, not just those on the fast track. Assignments that provide an opportunity to grow and to acquire new skills should be available to everyone.

Over the long run, companies have a lot to gain from encouraging career resilience. But there is also an immediate reason to adopt this approach: employees are beginning to demand it, say corporate leaders. People are angry these days when they find that they lack the skills needed to get another job. People are angry when their employers break the old covenant and offer nothing to take its place.

Awareness of that anger, plus an obsession with creating a "nimble organization" and a fervent belief in treating employees as respectworthy adults, prompted Sun to establish its career-resilience program in 1991. Like many Silicon Valley companies, Sun was in the midst of rethinking its businesses, reorganizing its manufacturing operations, and reexamining the makeup of its workforce. The result was little change in the overall number of employees but a big change in the composition of the workforce. While Sun added hundreds of sales representatives, it "redeployed" hundreds of manufacturing employees. That meant that their jobs were being phased out and they had to find other jobs in the company, if they could, or accept a severance package, which was what most had to do.

"We became convinced that we had a responsibility to put employees back in control of their lives," says Marianne F. Jackson, who was a human resources director at Sun when she came up with the idea for the career-resilience program. Jackson, who is now at another high-tech company, believes that organizations that replace the old covenant with one based on career resilience will have a dramatic edge. We do too. They will have an edge in attracting and retaining the best people. And they will have an edge in the struggle to develop the capabilities needed to compete tomorrow.

Today the handful of pioneering companies with career-resilience programs are still feeling their way forward, learning what works and what doesn't. But from the progress they've made so far, we can discern some basic ingredients all programs should include and some pitfalls to avoid.

The Basics of Career Resilience

One ingredient of a successful program is a system that helps employees regularly assess their skills, interests, values, and temperaments so that they can figure out the type of job for which they are best suited. Another is a system that enables employees to benchmark their skills on a regular basis. These systems help employees understand both themselves and the work to be done so well that, ideally, they routinely find their way into the right jobs and routinely update their skills. These systems help prod, awaken, and galvanize so that square pegs and round pegs find their way into the right holes. Imagine how productivity would soar if most people had jobs that turned them on!

By self-assessment, we mean a systematic process of taking stock of those attributes that influence one's effectiveness, success, and happiness. Unless individuals understand the environments that let them shine, the interests that ignite them, and the skills that help them excel, how can they choose a company or job where they can make their greatest contribution? Unless they understand how their personal style affects others, how can they function with maximum effectiveness? Knowing yourself is the first step toward becoming career resilient.

Take Frank Aragona of Raychem. Aragona was a high-level nonexempt employee in the customer-service department of a plant that manufactures heating cables. After eight years in the same functional area of the same plant, Aragona felt dead-ended. He had learned all he could and, he thought, risen as high as he could with Raychem. His choices seemed to be to leave or to stagnate.

Then Aragona began attending some lunchtime seminars at the company's new career center. Using the center's library and working with a career counselor on self-assessment, he confirmed a long-felt need for something new and different. He also realized something else: some of his career interests—for example, becoming a historian—were just plain unrealistic for him. "[The center] gave me a shot of reality and set things in perspective," he explains. Armed with better knowledge of himself, Aragona became interested when a coworker told him of a position in the international-sales division. It would build on his skills in customer service but offer new challenges, and the international aspect appealed to the explorer in him. He interviewed for the job and got it. He also got a promotion and a raise. Both Aragona and Raychem came out winners.

Companies certainly can encourage employees to assess themselves and can help them by providing the necessary tools. For some, self-assessment can be as simple as digesting a career-development book like Richard Nelson Bolles's *What Color Is Your Parachute?* or articulating their strengths and the value they can bring to a job. But most people will profit from a more thorough process. This may include tests—or "assessment instruments," as career-development professionals call them—designed to reveal an individual's motivations and interests (for example, the Myers-Briggs Type Indicator and the Strong Interest Inventory) and sessions with a counselor trained to interpret the results.

As we mentioned, the second step in the process of becoming career resilient is ensuring that one has competitive skills. Companies need to give employees the tools to benchmark their skills and experience with what the job market inside and outside the company is demanding.

We are not saying that a company should relinquish its right to judge what skills it needs in its workforce in order to be competitive, and what training that involves. What we are saying is that, *in addition,* all employees should have the right to demand the training and challenging work experiences they need to update their skills. They have a right to minimize the risk of winding up stuck in a dead-end or vulnerable job. In other words, employers and employees should be partners in the continuous process of benchmarking and updating skills.

The Company's Obligations

To enable employees to benchmark their skills, companies will have to be much more open with them than most have traditionally been. Management must maintain a continuing dialogue about the company's business direction and what is happening in its markets. How else can employees determine which skills the company will need down the road? How else can they decide whether they want to develop those skills—or prepare to leave? Managers have an obligation to give employees as much time as possible to prepare for the future. Sun's management has promised workers that when it comes to strategic decisions that affect jobs or careers (like outsourcing a function), "as soon as we've decided something, you'll know."

At 3Com, most departments hold weekly discussion sessions on the status of the business and its implications. Those sessions helped most of the 40 people in the

MIS department who supported 3Com's computer network to make the transition smoothly when 3Com changed the network operating system in April from 3+Open to Netware and Lotus Notes. They had long known that such a change was in the offing, that it would require them to get new skills or leave, and that the company would give them the time and resources to obtain the new skills. "The large majority were excited about making the change and getting the new skills," says Debra Engel, a 3Com vice president whose responsibilities include MIS and human resources. "Only a few departed—those who didn't want to make the change or didn't feel they could."

A company must help people explore opportunities, promote lifelong learning, and, if it comes to that, support no-fault exits.

A company must help people explore job opportunities, facilitate lifelong learning and job movement, and, if it comes to that, support no-fault exits. Raychem, for example, has created an insiders' network of more than 360 people throughout the organization who are willing to take the time to talk with any employee who wants to learn about the nature of their work and the requirements of their jobs. Their names and backgrounds are in a computerized database called I.I.I.N.siders (for Internal Information Interview Network). Apple lets people sample jobs by filling in for those taking the sabbatical that is available to all employees.

Most of the companies we studied make information on job openings inside and outside the organization available to all employees. In addition, they provide reference materials and training to help employees develop plans for professional growth and hone their résumé-writing and interviewing skills. They also bring in experts to speak about market trends. Such support, which can be made available at a "career center" or through a computer network connecting the company's operations, is essential. It not only helps employees find new jobs inside or, if need be, outside the organization but also enables them to benchmark their skills.

Companies and individuals often fail to realize that benchmarking without self-assessment may cause an employee to make the wrong choices. The experiences of an electrical engineer at a progressive high-tech company that lacked a bona fide career-resilience program demonstrate why. Through benchmarking, the engineer learned that the road to modest riches lay in project management. He took that road and was successful. But at the end of his typical 12-hour day as a project leader, he was completely stressed out. At home all he wanted to do was to curl up in a corner and read. "When I got home, I just didn't want to be with people," he says, adding that this situation certainly didn't help his marriage, which ended in divorce.

The problem was this: By nature he was something of a perfectionist who enjoyed working alone. Constantly having to work with others was simply not a good fit. He finally realized this after working as a project leader for six years and decided to go back to straight engineering. But he'd been away from it for so long that he needed to go back to school to catch up. His company fully supported his move; it even paid the tuition. The engineer is now much happier, and, at least in this instance, a company was able to keep a valued employee.

An employee's manager should not have the power to block a job transfer unilaterally.

Besides facilitating self-assessment and benchmarking, a company must make it easy for employees to learn and to become flexible. Workers should have the right to obtain ongoing training. Managers must be receptive to lateral transfers and even to employees' taking a step back to broaden their experience or to be happier and more productive. Indeed, an employee should have the right to switch jobs within the company, provided there is a need and he or she readily qualifies to fill it. An employee's manager should not have the power to block such a move unilaterally.

If an employee is not qualified for a desired job, then the company and the employee should jointly try to make the necessary training available. In some instances, the employee might take an in-house course on company time. In others, the company might help to pay for courses at a college or vocational school that the employee takes during his or her personal time.

For most companies, supporting each employee's need for lifelong learning will entail a greater commitment of time and resources to education. Raychem's Saldich passionately believes that it's not enough for an organization's leaders to make more resources available; they must campaign to get employees to use them. "I started out saying to people throughout Raychem that it's now okay to spend more time, money, and energy on learning," Saldich says. "After a year of that, I realized that saying it's okay is not good enough. Our philosophy now is that learning is mandatory and that every one of our people should have a learning or development plan."

Leaders elsewhere seem to agree. Executives from Motorola, who estimate that the company reaps a return of $33 for each dollar it spends on education, think that at least 5% of each employee's time should be spent on training or education. In his book *The Age of Unreason,* Charles Handy says that 20% is reasonable for managers. The "correct" percentage isn't important. (How do you measure it accurately? What about the value of special assignments that are both training and real work?) The point is that continuous learning is imperative, and the organization must be seen by its employees as committed to their development.

But employees must be aware that a shift in the company's direction may mean that the company, for justifiable reasons, suddenly will no longer need their skills. Similarly, people who decide to leave the organization should be able to depart with their heads held high. "The new covenant is about empowering people so they have job choices when circumstances change," says 3Com's Engel. "That's a lot healthier than the traditional blame relationship." Last and far from least among the company's obligations is to provide for no-fault exits.

Whether a departure is voluntary or involuntary, the company must support the affected employee in managing his or her transition. Kenneth M. Alvares, vice president for human resources at Sun Microsystems, puts it this way: "Companies ought to be able to figure out a way to manage all aspects of an employee's career with class or dignity. We do a great job of recruiting people. We also ought to do an equally great job of helping them to manage their careers while they're here. And when people find out it's time to leave this organization, we ought to handle that process with as much class as we do the recruiting process." Alvares does not just mean providing employees with the resources to make and implement a decision to leave. He also means continuing to treat them as valuable people. A company might even emphasize to departing employees that they will be welcomed back should their return serve the company's and their interests in the future.

Controlling the Risks

Creating a career-resilient workforce in the manner we have described is obviously easier said than done. "How can a company realistically give employees much greater freedom to demand new jobs and training?" skeptical managers will undoubtedly ask. "Won't it result in chaos? Isn't there a big danger that it will undermine productivity rather than increase it? Isn't it absurd to think that a company can put the career interests of an individual employee ahead of, say, getting a key product under development to market? And the notion of an insiders' network that will enable people to explore new jobs or careers might sound dandy, but how can we expect already overworked people to spend endless hours talking about what they do with employees in search of themselves?"

All those risks are real. But the short answer is that tomorrow's managers may have no choice. In this age of mobility, companies face even greater dangers if they do not commit themselves to developing self-reliant workers. They risk losing talented people who decide that the drawbacks of staying at such a company outweigh the rewards. This is already a big problem, managers tell us.

Consider the following story, which is replayed every day at scores of Silicon Valley companies. A gifted software engineer is an important member of a team that is developing a major new release of a workstation company's operating system. The engineer, who has been at the company for eight years, has worked on three previous releases and feels stale. In hunting around for a new challenge that will allow her to expand her skills, she discovers an opening in the division that is working on a decoder that the company hopes will give it a foothold in the emerging interactive-TV market.

The head of the division says he'd be thrilled to have her. But the manager of the release project doesn't want to let her go. Her departure will only make it more difficult for the team to meet its ambitious deadline. While interactive TV may be the big market of the future, there won't *be* a future if the workstation business continues to lose ground, he tells her. A month later, the engineer quits to join a start-up that is developing software for interactive TV. When the company's president learns about her departure, he is dismayed. "I would have overridden the project manager," he says. "If only I had known."

There is another element of our model that we know can make executives nervous: sharing sensitive information with employees. For example, conventional wisdom holds that a company has much to lose and little to gain by telling employees as soon as it has decided to exit a business or shut down an operation. The assumption is that morale and productivity will suffer, people will abandon ship, and the performance of the operation will quickly deteriorate, hurting the company and reducing the operation's value to a potential buyer.

Companies that share sensitive information say employees appreciate being treated as adults and respond in kind.

But executives at such companies as Sun, Apple, and 3Com don't think there is a choice. By not sharing such information, a company perpetuates the traditional parent-child relationship with employees, which is no longer tenable, they say. Companies that do share information say that employees have appreciated being treated as adults and have responded in kind. That is what happened with 3Com's buildings-management function, which the company outsourced last year.

In 1992, when 3Com decided to analyze whether it should outsource the function, the company immediately informed the unit's 35 employees. 3Com told them that the decision would take about nine months to make, invited their input, and promised to give them monthly updates. The company also said that if it did decide to go with outside vendors, the employees would have two weeks to decide whether to take two months' severance pay or a temporary position that would tide them over until they found another job inside or outside 3Com. Most of the employees stayed until the end and took the severance pay. But even the few who didn't stick it out kept 3Com informed of their plans so that the company had time to figure out how to manage without them. "It is no coincidence that we were very open with them and they were very open with us," Engel says.

Once organizations accept the inevitability of change, there are systems they can put in place to minimize the risks involved in adopting career-resilience programs. At 3Com, for example, when an employee deemed critical by his or her current manager requests a transfer to an available job, the transfer cannot be denied but the date of the transfer can be negotiated. "If managers resist," says Engel, "they're reminded, 'You'd find an answer if that employee quit tomorrow.' There's always an answer."

> *Unless employees are convinced that a career-resilience program truly is there to serve them, they won't participate in it.*

Raychem and Apple have devised a way to prevent their information networks from consuming much of the time of valuable, overworked employees. They ask people throughout the company to volunteer to give informational interviews. When someone signs up, he or she agrees to do a certain number. Afterward, the person has the option of doing a certain number more or dropping out.

In fact, managers themselves have a lot to gain by participating in such networks. Informational networking enables them to get a look at a broader set of people than they otherwise would in the normal course of their work. As they form task forces or look for people to fill vacant slots, they have more potential candidates. And this process can help their organization achieve something that is increasingly hard to do in this era of churning workforces: build a sense of community.

Gaining Credibility

Unless employees are convinced that a career-resilience program truly is there to serve their interests, they simply won't participate in it. Establishing a career-management center helps a program gain credibility. Sun, Raychem, and Apple have set up such centers as havens where employees can go to work on self-assessment, receive counseling, and attend seminars on, say, how to conduct an effective job interview or how to network. They are places where employees can obtain career reference materials, check on internal and external job openings, contribute to discussions on business strategy, and, most important, learn how to think strategically about their own careers.

The center's location is very important. By making it highly visible and easily accessible, the company sends the message that it is not only acceptable but desirable for employees to use it. The opposite message may be sent by locating it off the beaten track. Raychem and Sun are considering opening satellite centers for employees at other operations who cannot easily use the companies' single centers. Another idea is mobile centers that can serve several sites.

Sun and Apple also use their centers for outplacement. But before doing so, companies should carefully consider the trade-offs, according to several executives. The advantages are that the skills and resources needed for career development and outplacement overlap, and that the dual role makes the center easier to justify financially.

The disadvantage is that, especially in the beginning, employees might infer that the career-resilience program is an outplacement program in disguise—and misinterpret the message when management encourages them to use the center. For that reason, Raychem does not use its center, which opened last September, for outplacement; its sole mission is to enhance career resilience.

To allay employees' initial fears, several companies urge managers to encourage their employees to use the center, but they make it clear that managers do not have the right to know if they have gone there, let alone what transpired. Also, to assure employees that the purpose of the program is to help them manage their careers and not to help their superiors manage them, these companies believe that the career-management process must be separate from the regular performance-appraisal process.

The human dimension is perhaps the most crucial element of any career-resilience program. It is hard to imagine a successful program without counselors and career-research specialists to add a personal touch. Without them, many employees will not be able to use the information effectively; many probably won't even bother to try. Sun, Raychem, and Apple seem to understand that. At their centers, as soon as people walk in, they encounter specialists whose job is to teach them how to use the facilities.

But employees have to believe that the counselor represents their interests. Confidentiality is an obvious concern for people thinking about changing jobs or employers. It is difficult but not impossible for a staff counselor to gain an employee's trust. For example, Carol Dunne, the counselor at Apple's Career Resource Center, has earned such a reputation. But as one manager who uses outside career counselors puts it, "Employees often believe that the human resources department represents management's interests, not theirs." Using outside career counselors can help convince employees that the program really is there to serve them.

There is another advantage to using outside counselors: it can be more cost-effective. Several pioneers in developing career-resilient workers have taken this course.

Sun, Apple, and Raychem have turned to the Career Action Center, a nonprofit organization in Palo Alto, California. Formed in the early 1970s to provide career advice to women in Silicon Valley, the center has become a major institution in the area, serving thousands of Silicon Valley workers. While Sun's, Apple's, and Raychem's career centers are headed by their own employees, the staffs include career-research specialists and counselors from the Career Action Center. The mix of insiders and outsiders makes a powerful combination: the insiders know the company's culture, networks, and operations, and the outsiders bring special expertise, objectivity, and cost flexibility.

Taking the idea of partnership a step further, several midsize Silicon Valley companies led by 3Com are studying the idea of forming a consortium to provide career-resilience services to all their employees. The other companies include Quantum, Aspect Telecommunications, Novell, Octel Communications, Silicon Graphics, Claris, and ESL. There are several reasons why this idea appeals to them. One is that the consortium could afford to provide more services than each company could on its own. A second is that the companies could learn from one another. Finally, an operation relatively immune to the politics and financial ups and downs of any one company might be better able to serve its customers: the employees. The flip side is that it might be harder to integrate such a shared center into each company's mainstream operations.

Some companies, most notably Apple, are using technology to make career-resilience programs widely available and part of the mainstream. Apple is placing large amounts of career information on its "electronic campus," the computer network that ties together its operations. By strolling the right digital paths on the campus, individuals can find a "resource and referral" section that includes lists of books, professional associations, conferences, courses, articles, and other information that Apple employees recommend to their coworkers.

The big advantage of an electronic network over a career center is, of course, accessibility. All employees in Apple's far-flung global operations will have equal access to career-related information. Moreover, computer systems are private, available at the convenience of the user, and easy to update. The danger is that companies and people will become so absorbed by the technology that they will lose sight of the importance of the human dimension. Computer networks may be a superior way to make data widely available. But for individuals trying to remain employable and for executives trying to keep the organization competitive, the patterns and analysis that give meaning to the data are the most valuable tools. And it usually takes personal interactions for them to emerge.

Support from the Top

It almost goes without saying that a career-resilience program won't even get off the ground without visible support from the top. Without the backing of top management, it is implausible to think that managers down the ranks will consistently share with employees their knowledge about strategy and market conditions so that employees can anticipate the company's needs and make career decisions.

Raychem's policy is to try to find places inside the company for employees in dead-end jobs.

Nor is it plausible to assume that most managers will automatically buy into the notion that employees should be the eyes and ears of the company, that all employees can and should help shape strategy. There is still too much tradition to be overcome.

Among the companies we studied, Raychem stands out in terms of top management's visible commitment. At the opening ceremony for the career center, Harry O.

Postlewait, the company's executive vice president, spoke, and he made sure the audience knew that the CEO, Bob Saldich, would have been there, too, had he not been at home in bed with the flu. Several senior executives, including Saldich, are in the database of people who volunteered to be interviewed by anyone in the company seeking career information.

Saldich and other senior Raychem executives seem to realize that to cultivate a sense of community in a company, management must show that it genuinely cares about its people—even those who have left. That is why Raychem's policy is to try to find places inside the company for those in dead-end jobs or in need of development, to use outplacement only as the last resort, and to tell talented people who leave that they will be welcomed back if possible. This type of caring approach is the only way an organization can get employees to believe that its fate is their responsibility, not just that of top management. It's a new basis for loyalty in today's transient world. Potentially it's a great competitive advantage.

But for a company to reap the full benefits of a career-resilience program, the program must be consistent with and supported by the other elements of the company's business and human resources strategies. There must be systems to support the approach—like a pay system that rewards flexibility, not position in the hierarchy, and flexible work arrangements so that employees have time to improve their skills.

Contrast Raychem with another company we know of that has attracted a lot of naturally self-reliant people. Its top management has yet to prove that it is genuinely committed to helping employees become career resilient, however. While the company generously supports education and training, many of its employees feel that top management doesn't really care whether they stay or leave. And top management gets poor grades on keeping employees informed about the company's business direction and enlisting them in shaping strategy. No wonder employees, when surveyed, cited career development as their main concern.

At some companies, the conviction that helping employees become career resilient should be a top priority still seems largely confined to the human resources department. That's a good start. But the responsibility for building a career-resilient workforce is too important to be relegated to any one department over the long run. That is why the early converts must include top management—so that the conversion process will continue down the ranks until everyone in the company is a believer. This is the approach that has been taken at Raychem. Its human resources department, the original champion, sees itself as a partner with operating management in the effort to create a companywide career-resilience program.

Of course, we realize that many operating managers are lamenting that their jobs are already impossible. On the one hand, the manager is supposed to be the coach, the coordinator, the conductor, and the team leader who supports, advises, and cheers on others so *they* can carry out the task. On the other hand, the manager is still the one held accountable for the final results. "How can you heap even more contradictions and uncertainty on us?" some have said in reaction to our ideas.

The answer is that this is an age of perhaps unprecedented uncertainty. Those managers who excel at juggling all the contradictions and uncertainties—who figure out how to harness the potentially awesome power of today's mobile workforce—will be the ones whose organizations will prevail in the marketplace.

On a less lofty level, managers have much to gain personally for two reasons. First, the career-resilience approach gives them a way to deal with an increasingly common phenomenon: the employee who is extremely distressed about his or her job—because the job is vulnerable, because it is no longer challenging, or because it offers no advancement opportunities. Second, career resilience is for managers too! Understanding themselves will help them be more effective managers. And by understanding themselves and benchmarking their own skills, managers—like all workers—will be better equipped to manage their own careers.

More than ever, the manager is responsible for creating an environment in which all employees have opportunities to develop so they do not hit a dead end, so their skills remain competitive. This means three things: keeping employees fully informed about the direction of the business; helping each employee understand that the responsibility for ensuring that he or she has competitive skills is ultimately the employee's; and abiding by the employee's right to be a free agent.

The switch from career dependence to career resilience is not only imperative but also inevitable. The company that recognizes this sea change and rides the waves has a huge strategic advantage. Such a company can be swift without being ruthless. It can encourage people to grow, to change, and to learn, and in doing so it becomes better at those things itself. Career resilience replaces a covenant we can no longer keep with one that is in everyone's best interest.

Originally published in July–August 1994
Reprint 94409

A Market-Driven Approach to Retaining Talent

PETER CAPPELLI

Executive Summary

OPEN COMPETITION FOR other companies' people, once a rarity in business, is now an accepted fact. Fast-moving markets require fast-moving organizations that are continually refreshed with new talent. But no one likes to see talent leave; when a good employee walks, the business takes a hit. It's futile to hope that by tinkering with compensation, career paths, and training efforts, you can wall off your company from today's labor market.

But there is an alternative: a market-driven approach to retention based on the assumption that long-term, across-the-board loyalty is neither possible nor desirable. By taking a hard look at which employees you need to retain and for how long, you can use highly targeted programs to keep the required talent in place.

Most companies today rely on compensation to build loyalty, but compensation is only one of many useful retention mechanisms. You can redesign jobs to reduce turnover: UPS kept many more drivers by shifting the tedious job of loading trucks to other employees. You can promote loyalty to particular projects or to work teams. You can hire people who aren't in high demand and place valuable employees in locations where they won't be constantly tempted by job offers. You can team up with other companies to offer cross-company career paths. And when there's no effective way to prevent attrition, you can learn to live with it: outsource, strengthen recruitment, standardize jobs, cross-train employees, and organize work around short-term projects.

If managing retention in the past was akin to tending a dam, today it is more like managing a river. The object is not to stop water from flowing but to control its direction and speed.

IF YOU'RE LIKE MOST EXECUTIVES today, you're a poacher. You regularly look outside your organization to find talented individuals to fill key posts. And when you spot attractive candidates, you do what it takes to lure them away from their current employers. You offer big signing bonuses, you buy out stock options, and you provide rich compensation packages of your own. All the while, you know that other companies are busily rifling through your own organization, hoping to poach your best talent.

The open competition for other companies' people, once a rarity in business, is now an accepted fact. Executives know that fast-moving markets require fast-moving organizations that are continually refreshed with new talent, and they've become adept at outside hiring. (See "Strategic Poaching" at the end of this article.) But if they're comfortable bringing talent in, they remain distinctly uncomfortable about seeing talent leave. To poach is fine; to be poached is not. One reason for the discomfort is emotional. Executives tend to judge themselves on their ability to instill loyalty in their people, and the departure of a talented employee can feel like a personal affront. Another reason is rational. In a time of tight labor markets, talent can be very hard—and very expensive—to replace. When a good employee walks, the business takes a hit.

In trying to stop people from jumping ship, many companies have fallen back on traditional retention programs. I recently attended a talk by a senior manager from DuPont who was telling of a corporate initiative to "re-engage" with employees. By designing and promoting new, long-term career paths and investing heavily in employee development, the company hoped to win back the loyalty of its workforce. When a member of the audience asked him if he really thought the company could stop the outflow of talent, the speaker replied, in a moment of unexpected candor, that he did not—the competition was simply too intense. But, he went on, the company's executives saw no alternative. They had to make the effort.

The speaker was right about one thing. It is futile to hope that by tinkering with compensation programs, career paths, training efforts, and the like, a company can insulate itself from today's freewheeling labor market. That doesn't mean, however, that companies should just go through the motions. There is an alternative: a market-driven retention strategy that begins with the assumption that long-term, across-the-board employee loyalty is neither possible nor desirable. The focus shifts from broad retention programs to highly targeted efforts aimed at particular employees or groups of employees. Moving to a market-driven strategy is not easy. It requires executives to take a hard-headed, analytical approach to what has long been viewed as a "soft" side of business—the management of people. But it is necessary. The clock can't be turned back.

Rethinking Retention

To adopt the new strategy, you first have to accept the new reality: the market, not your company, will ultimately determine the movement of your employees. Yes, you can make your organization as pleasant and rewarding a place to work in as possible—you can fix problems that may push people toward the exits. But you can't counter the pull of the market; you can't shield your people from attractive opportunities and aggressive recruiters. The old goal of HR management—to minimize overall employee turnover—needs to be replaced by a new goal: to influence who leaves and when. If managing employee retention in the past was akin to tending a dam that keeps a reservoir in place, today it is more like managing a river. The object is not to prevent water from flowing out but to control its direction and its speed.

Prudential is one company that has begun to adopt this market-driven perspective. Its "Building Management Capability" program, which integrates recruiting, retention, and training efforts, is geared toward an increasingly mobile workforce. "Gone is the notion that employees are going to stay with one company for life," says Kurt Metzger, a human resources executive at the company. The Prudential program is anchored by a sophisticated planning model that projects talent requirements and attrition rates. The model enables business-unit managers to develop highly targeted retention programs and create cost-effective contingency plans for filling potential gaps in skills. The model also provides a mechanism for constantly measuring the impact of human resources decisions, a capability crucial to managing people in this rapidly shifting labor market.

Prudential has begun doing what most companies avoid: making a truly honest assessment of how long the organization would like employees to stay on board. Such an analysis inevitably reveals that different groups of employees warrant very different retention efforts. There will always be some people a company will want to keep indefinitely—an engineering genius, an inspiring business head, a creative product designer, or a frontline worker deeply respected by customers. Another set of people will be important to retain for shorter, well-defined periods—employees with specific skills that are currently in short supply, for instance, or members of a team creating a new product or installing a new information system. And finally there will be people for whom investments in retention don't make sense—employees in easy-to-fill jobs that require little training or employees whose skills aren't in demand in the market.

Once you know which employees you need to retain and for how long, you can use a number of mechanisms to encourage them to stay. The key is to resist the temptation to use the mechanisms across the board. Tailor your programs to your retention requirements for various employees and to the level of demand for them in the marketplace. Let's look at some of the mechanisms and their strengths and shortcomings.

COMPENSATION

The most popular retention mechanism today is compensation. Most companies try to lock in their most valuable employees with "golden handcuffs"—pay packages weighted heavily toward unvested options or other forms of deferred compensation. The problem with pay-based incentives is that they're easy for outsiders to match. Recruiters routinely buy out golden handcuffs with signing bonuses—"golden hellos." Retention incentives end up becoming just another element of compensation, contributing more to wage inflation than to long-term retention. (See "The Futility of Golden Handcuffs" at the end of this article.)

But compensation can help shape who leaves and when. Some companies now pay special "hot skills" premiums to employees whose expertise is crucial and in short supply. The payments are an effective way to keep talent in place for critical periods, such as through the late stages of the design of an important product. The premiums cease the minute the skills become more readily available on the market or the employer decides that the skills are no longer as important to its business. Andersen Consulting, for example, recently eliminated its hot-skills premium for SAP programmers.

Paying signing bonuses in stages, rather than as lump sums, can also help to keep new employees in place, at least in the short run. Deferred signing bonuses are becoming the norm for executive-level hires. When Associated Communications (now Teligent) gave Alex Mandl, AT&T's heir apparent, a $20 million signing bonus to become its new CEO, it paid out the money over five years. Such bonuses are proving useful in retaining lower-level employees as well. Burger King, for example, offers workers a signing bonus but withholds payment until they've been on the job for three months. Three months may not seem like a long time, but in the fast-food business, where annual turnover averages 300%, it's an eternity.

A deferred bonus doesn't guarantee that a new employee will stay for the deferment period, of course. Such incentives are, after all, just a form of golden handcuffs. Another company can always come along with a big golden hello.

JOB DESIGN

To retain people with critical skills for longer periods, companies need better mechanisms than compensation. One is job design. By thinking carefully about which tasks to include in which jobs, companies can exert considerable influence over retention rates.

Consider what United Parcel Service did to improve its retention of drivers. UPS recognized that drivers have some of the most important skills in the delivery business. They know the idiosyncrasies of the routes and they have direct relationships with customers. Finding, screening, and training a replacement driver is time consuming; it may take a new hire months to learn the details of a particular route.

UPS targeted skills it wanted to retain; for workers without them, it allowed the revolving door to spin freely.

When UPS studied the reasons its drivers left, it discovered that much of the turnover could be traced to the tedious and exhausting task of loading packages at the beginning of a run. It therefore unbundled the loading task from the drivers' job and assigned it to a new group of workers. The turnover rate for drivers fell dramatically.

Of course, turnover in the new loading jobs averages an eye-popping 400% per year. But that doesn't matter. With high hourly wages and low skill requirements, the loading jobs are fairly easy for UPS to fill, typically with students or other part-timers, and fairly simple for new employees to learn. A high turnover rate in the loading jobs is expected and manageable. In using job design to improve retention, UPS didn't attempt to decrease overall turnover; instead, it targeted the specific skills it wanted to retain. For employees without those skills, it allowed the revolving door to spin freely.

Jobs can also be defined in such a way as to influence when people will leave. Wall Street investment firms were once plagued by erratic, unplanned turnover among junior analysts. The companies addressed the problem by requiring the analysts to leave after three years. Forcing people to quit may seem like an odd way to solve a turnover problem, but it makes a lot of sense. The real issue, after all, was not that the junior analysts were leaving—it was expected that many would go on to business school—but that the firms could not predict who would leave or when. As a result, project teams were often left understaffed, leading to delays and quality problems. Now that they know junior analysts will depart at the end of their third year, the firms can design projects to coincide with analysts' tenures. Having clear termination dates also creates large, well-defined employee cohorts, making training and development easier. The emergence of the three-year stint as an industry standard helps ensure that employees stay for the full period because a junior-analyst job lasting less than three years looks bad on a résumé.

JOB CUSTOMIZATION

In addition to tailoring jobs to particular categories of employees, companies can also tailor them to the needs of individuals. Prudential is experimenting with such a program. It provides workers with a variety of tools to help them assess their own interests, values, and skills, and it encourages managers to tailor rewards, benefits, and assignments to individual requirements. A part-time arrangement might satisfy one employee's desire to pursue outside interests or meet a parenting need, while tuition reimbursement might be the key to keeping another employee happy.

Prudential's program draws on an array of employment options, most of which are available to all workers. It's easy to imagine, however, programs that would go even further in customizing jobs. Key employees might undertake a formal self-assessment of their work and nonwork goals and of how those goals could best be achieved in the context of the company's operations. The assessments would form the basis for individual employment agreements, which might be created using cafeteria-style programs similar to those used in allocating employee benefits. Each employee would be able to allocate a set amount of money to "purchase" options in such areas as career development and balancing work and personal life. The amount available to allocate would depend on the importance of the employee to the company.

Individualized deals always raise fairness concerns, of course. Basing rewards on skills, rather than just on performance, is something new, and it's sure to rub some people the wrong way. But there are plenty of precedents. Salaries have long been based on the labor market—those in hot fields get paid more. Relative compensation routinely hinges on criteria outside an employee's control, such as the performance of a division or the state of the stock market. And most companies have always had a fast-track career path for employees deemed more valuable than their peers on measures other than current job performance. Giving greater benefits to those with critical skills that are difficult to replace seems in tune with these established practices.

The bigger issue may lie with the form of the rewards rather than in how they are distributed. Few companies allow employees to design their own jobs, and those that do usually offer such programs across the board rather than selectively. That's the case, for example, with most flextime arrangements. Companies will need to consider carefully the effects on morale as well as the legal implications of selective programs, but they should not reject them simply because they're unusual and raise tough questions. The market is very creative in providing individualized rewards. Companies should be equally creative.

SOCIAL TIES

Loyalty to companies may be disappearing, but loyalty to colleagues is not. By encouraging the development of social ties among key employees, companies can often significantly reduce turnover among workers whose skills are in high demand. Carl Glaeser, general manager of Ingage Solutions, a Phoenix-based division of AG Communication Systems, has held the turnover of software engineers to 7%, mainly by developing programs that create a social community in the workplace. Golf leagues, investment clubs, and softball squads create social ties and bind workers to their current jobs. Leaving the company means leaving your social network of company-sponsored activities.

Arrangements that help create community within an organization have one big potential drawback: they make the trauma of any eventual restructuring all the more intense. Creating strong social ties is therefore inappropriate for employees who are likely to become less vital to a company in the near future. But you can achieve a similar bonding effect, minus the long-term complications, with teams. By creating closely knit teams to carry out particular projects, companies can increase the likelihood that the teams will remain intact for the length of the initiatives. People who would hardly think twice about abandoning a company find it very difficult to walk out on their teammates. Teams also have an added benefit: studies have shown that they increase employees' commitment to their work. (See "Commitment Without Loyalty" at the end of this article.)

When companies recruit, they often focus on attracting precisely those people who will be the most difficult to retain.

LOCATION

Large businesses have another good mechanism for managing retention: location. By carefully choosing the sites for various groups of employees, they can influence turnover rates. A high-tech company, for example, might find it useful to have a research and development operation in Silicon Valley in order to tap into cutting-edge thinking. The inevitable high turnover rate will be an advantage: the company will be exposed to a broad array of ideas. But an R&D project with a long lead time could be doomed by such high turnover. The company would be wise to set up a long-term R&D operation in a place where the skills of the development team are not in high demand, such as a rural community. People will still leave from time to time, but overall turnover will be much lower. At a Harris Semiconductor (now Intersil) facility in rural Pennsylvania, turnover recently averaged just 2% a year, far below the 20% average for the semiconductor industry.

Of course, trying to get people to relocate to remote regions poses its own challenges. But here again it makes sense to think about the individual circumstances and needs of your people. Employees who have young families, for instance, may be very interested in moving to a smaller, more rural community. Once they're there, it will be hard for them to pull up stakes and leave.

HIRING

When companies go out recruiting, they often focus on attracting precisely those people who will be the most difficult to retain. By shifting their sights to workers who can do the job but are not in high demand, organizations may be able to shelter themselves from market forces. Microboard Processing, a Connecticut-based assembler of electronic components, hires one-third of its assemblers from high-risk applicants, including welfare recipients, former drug addicts, and people with criminal records. The company often starts the new recruits on simple landscaping jobs to see how they do before moving them inside to the assembly operation. It also gives them lots of slack during the first few months on the job while they are growing used to the discipline of factory work. In return, the company says it is getting a hard-working pool of employees who are grateful and loyal to Microboard for giving them a chance.

Architectural Support Services, a computer-aided-design company providing technical support for architects, also uses hiring to bolster retention. In its early days, the company followed textbook HR practices, hiring the best and brightest professionals available. Yet it found its operations in shambles because of poor morale and high turnover—all caused by infighting among the high-powered staff. The company thought hard about its workforce and realized that it did not need to fill all its positions with gifted workers. It started recruiting from community colleges instead of elite four-year institutions. The company has been rewarded with a much more loyal and committed workforce—and its results have not suffered in the least.

Adapting to Attrition

Sometimes there will be no effective way to ensure the retention of a particular employee or group of employees. The market forces will be too strong. Look at the trouble companies have holding on to their information technologists. The extremely tight labor market gives talented techies a wealth of opportunities, and the field's rapidly changing skill requirements give them an incentive to seek new projects that will advance their expertise. Companies with a strong need to retain particular IT skills—for maintaining legacy systems, say—are in a bind. Their best course is often to avoid the retention issue altogether by outsourcing the required skills. J.P.

Morgan is among the many companies that have taken the outsourcing route. It collaborated with several IT companies to establish Pinnacle Alliance, which now manages Morgan's global IT operations. Morgan found that the best way to deal with an intractable skill shortage is to let somebody else deal with it.

In other cases, companies have found that high turnover isn't as big a problem as it appears. Just because a business is dependent on engineering skills, for example, doesn't mean that it has to go to great lengths to retain its engineers. If there's a large pool of engineers available, it might want to focus on recruitment rather than retention. That's exactly what a number of electronics companies in Ireland have been doing. Irish universities are producing a steady supply of talented engineers trained in the latest technologies. The electronics companies recruit aggressively at these schools, but they make relatively little effort to retain their current engineers. That way, they continually infuse their organizations with the most up-to-date skills. Moreover, since new hires have lower salaries than longer-term employees, the companies are able to keep a lid on compensation levels.

There are also ways to adapt organizations and operations to high turnover. Simplifying and standardizing jobs and cross-training workers in multiple jobs make companies less dependent on any one individual. Many semiconductor companies, for example, have responded to high turnover rates among machine operators by certifying operators on more machines and rotating them to new positions every three months or so. Moving from legacy systems, even if they suit the organization's needs, to more common, off-the-shelf systems helps ensure that needed skills will be readily available in the marketplace. And organizing work around short-term projects with clear end points can make turnover easier to manage. Companies can focus their retention efforts on keeping employees just until a project is completed—a much easier task than building long-term loyalty.

Information technology can also help employers cope with turnover by preserving some of the institutional memory that employees would otherwise take with them. Customer relationship software automates sales and gives clerks access to client histories, including prior orders and complaints, allowing the clerks to sound familiar with accounts they know

Sometimes it's impossible to ensure the retention of a particular group of employees; in those cases, companies can learn to adapt.

nothing about. Groupware applications like Lotus Notes can standardize interactions and keep records of decisions and crucial contextual information, providing something like an electronic record of employee knowledge. Other programs, such as Open Text's Livelink, enable all employees to track and share documents on an intranet. New simulation software for team-based project management, such as Thinking Tools' Project Challenge, helps new teams learn how to work together much more quickly than on-the-job experience would allow.

Even a technology as simple as e-mail can prove to be a godsend when key employees are lost, as Pamela Hirshman, a project manager at Young & Rubicam, recently found out. She was called in to take over a project after the entire original project team had left. "The project file had a record of all the e-mails between the team and the client," she says, "and after reviewing about 50 of these, I was up to speed on the problems of the client and where the project was heading."

Cooperating with Competitors

Because of the intensity of the talent war, companies instinctively view retention and recruitment as competitive exercises—a perspective that has kept them from seeking help from one another. But history shows that cooperation, even among competitors, can be one of the most effective ways of dealing with talent shortages. In the 1950s, the big aircraft companies like Lockheed, McDonnell-Douglas, and Northrop competed fiercely for the government contracts that were their lifeblood. When a company won a new contract, it faced the challenge of quickly hiring skilled staff to carry out the work. When a company lost a contract or simply finished a project, it had the problem of excess staff.

A solution emerged in southern California, where many of the companies had operations. They began to "lend" teams of employees to one another. A company that lost a fighter contract, for example, would hire out a team of experienced employees to the company that won it. The team members would remain employees of the first company. Lockheed reported that its program, known as Lending Employees for National Development (LEND), had a wide range of benefits. In addition to avoiding layoffs, the company retained its investment in key employees, maintained its capability to bid on future contracts, and broadened the experience of its leased employees.

The aerospace industry saw another type of cooperation, one between prime contractors and subcontractors.

Complicated components for large projects would be created at a subcontractor, then moved to the prime contractor, where they were assembled into a larger module and passed on to a final assembler before being delivered to a client like NASA—a process that could take years. Key employees of the subcontractor followed the component to the prime contractor, becoming employees of the prime contractor and working alongside its staff.

Perhaps the most expansive current example of cooperation in hiring is the Talent Alliance, which began at AT&T and has grown to include about 30 large companies. It started as a kind of sophisticated job bank during the era of downsizing and high unemployment. Companies that had to lay off skilled workers could market them to other employers that might be looking for such skills. The Talent Alliance has since expanded its charter. It now provides standardized tests for screening and evaluating people and for matching them with jobs at member firms.

Other, more ad hoc, collaborations are appearing among noncompeting companies. Cascade Engineering, a plastic parts manufacturer in Grand Rapids, Michigan, has teamed up with a local Burger King to coordinate recruiting. Applicants who do not have the skills necessary for Cascade's production positions but who otherwise seem like good workers are offered jobs at Burger King. Successful Burger King employees who begin looking for more skilled positions are offered vocational counseling at Cascade. The prospect of moving to Cascade provides an incentive for people to join and stick with Burger King, and the Burger King employees become a dependable labor pool for Cascade. The career development that individuals in the past would have experienced within a single company now takes place across two companies.

Cooperating with other companies to develop employees and lay out possible career paths goes against the grain of traditional HR management, which is based on the assumption that employees are captive and proprietary assets. But it is in tune with the current reality of the market-driven workforce. One thing is for sure: as the early years of our new century unfold, executives will be challenged to abandon their old ways of thinking and adopt ever more creative ways of managing, retaining, and, yes, releasing their talent. Those who begin that difficult process now will be one step ahead of the game.

Strategic Poaching

THE SIGNS OF AN explosion in outside hiring are everywhere. The executive-search arm of A.T. Kearney reported that the number of searches undertaken by its clients in 1997 was 15% higher than in 1996, which was itself a record year, and that CEO searches were up 28%. When one St. Louis headhunter, John R. Sibbald, tracked the careers of 150 up-and-coming executives, he found that within two years, 80% had changed employers. Job fairs, once mainly nonprofit, informal events, have turned into highly profitable extravaganzas run by specialized companies that charge up to $5,000 per recruiting company. And electronic job markets, unknown a couple of years ago, are overflowing with recruiters and résumés.

One reason poaching has spread so rapidly is that companies have learned to use outside hiring strategically as well as tactically. They bring in experienced people not just to fill open positions but also to get the expertise they need to quickly expand into new markets or even to launch new businesses. As the consumer electronics and computer industries have moved into each other's markets, for example, they have begun to recruit each other's employees as a way to tap into each other's expertise. The U.S. unit of Mitsubishi's consumer electronics group recently hired 20 engineers from computer companies for its research staff in one swoop. "What you have is the NFL draft of electronics executives," says Bob Lee, head of Manpower Staffing Services in San Jose, California.

The strategic use of outside hiring is not limited to the volatile high-tech industry. Today when an oil company wants to expand the sales of products at its service stations, it hires managers from Pepsi and Frito-Lay with expertise in retailing. When an airline wants to get better at managing customer relationships, it recruits executives from Marriott with experience in customer service. When a power company prepares for deregulation, it hires people from a phone company that has already gone through the transition. Businesses have found that it's quicker to steal new competencies than to develop them from scratch.

Poaching can also provide a relatively easy way for companies to move into new regions. In 1995, Ernst & Young built up its presence in Spain by recruiting nearly the entire Madrid office of its competitor Coopers & Lybrand—90 people in all. When Allegheny Health Systems moved into the Philadelphia market in the mid-1990s, it raided the cardiology and cardiac surgery departments of Presbyterian Medical Center to develop an instant presence in those specialties. Presbyterian then turned around and hired all but one of the cardiologists from Cooper Health Systems in nearby Camden, New Jersey.

Hiring outside executives is now even seen as an effective, and frequently less risky, alternative to acquiring entire companies. A few years ago, AT&T wanted to enter the computer-systems-integration business, but it worried about whether it could incorporate an entire company into its culture. Instead, it asked recruiters to find the top 50 system integrators in the country. AT&T hired them and started its own systems-integration operations.

It would be a mistake to look at all this activity and think it's a passing phenomenon—a symptom of the booming economy and the tight labor market. The underlying changes in business are fundamental, not transient, and the use of outside hiring as a strategic tool will only grow in the future. While the overall demand for labor will rise and fall, the war for talent will rage on.

The Futility of Golden Handcuffs

TODAY VIRTUALLY EVERY company offers its key people some form of deferred compensation in hopes of buying their loyalty. When such golden-handcuffs programs were new, they effectively kept corporate recruiters at bay. Just as burglar alarms redistribute burglary to unprotected homes, golden handcuffs redistributed poaching to unprotected businesses. Some companies, like Emerson Electric, became famous for the elegance and elaborateness of their handcuffs.

But now that almost all companies offer their key people some form of deferred compensation, golden handcuffs are no longer a deterrent. With no unprotected companies left to pilfer from, recruiters have been forced to unlock the handcuffs by offering huge signing bonuses. In 1996, Alex Mandl, who appeared to be next in line for the CEO job at AT&T, was lured away to Associated Communications, a small operation that offered him a signing bonus of more than $20 million, much of which simply offset the $10 million in AT&T stock options he forfeited on leaving. No matter how generous the deferred compensation package you offer to one of your stars, there will always be another, more desperate company willing to pay even more.

In addition to being ineffective, golden-handcuffs programs sometimes backfire. When Lou Gerstner arrived at IBM in 1993, he discovered that despite all the unvested stock options the company offered, his key employees were being picked off by competitors right and left. The reason was the decline in IBM's stock price over the preceding years. The options had been rendered worthless, to the disgruntlement of employees. As Gerstner put it in a *Fortune* interview, "What I've got is an employee group with absolutely no incentive to stay here because every one of their options is under water."

Researchers have identified other perverse effects of golden handcuffs. A study of the semiconductor industry found that when large profit-sharing bonuses were distributed or when a company's stock price was booming, engineers often cashed in their profits and left to start their own businesses. That finding dovetails with a conclusion reached by labor economists: when employees get big windfalls, they tend to work less, essentially buying more leisure by retiring early or shifting to easier jobs with shorter hours.

At best ineffective, at worst counterproductive, deferred-compensation programs are nonetheless a necessity in business today. Since all companies offer them, your company will have to as well. The market demands it, and the market rules.

Commitment Without Loyalty

EXECUTIVES HAVE LONG SEEN loyalty and commitment as two sides of the same coin, believing that employees who lack loyalty to a company must also lack commitment to their work. From that perspective, the erosion of employee loyalty looks very scary. Research, after all, has shown a strong correlation between commitment and performance. If your employees lack commitment, you're in big trouble.

But there are many ways to engender commitment to the work without requiring loyalty to the company. Organizing work around projects is one such method. Studies have shown that when employees have control over a piece of work, they have greater commitment to seeing it done well. If it goes well, they get the credit, which increases their prestige (and helps build their résumés); if it fails, their reputations take a hit.

Creating teams is another way to build commitment. After all, commitment is far easier to establish among individuals than between an individual and an abstract entity such as a corporation. Team members work hard because they do not want to let the rest of the team down. The more accountable a team is for its performance, the greater the peer pressure on members to make sacrifices for the team. Team-based compensation, in particular, helps create the sense that the fate of the community relies on the performance of its members.

Even in industries long characterized by hostile relations between employees and employers, such as the U.S. auto industry, the redesign of production work around teams has contributed to sharp improvements in quality and overall performance, at least in part by engendering greater worker commitment.

The confusion of loyalty and commitment underlies another widely held but false belief: that commitment can exist only in a long-term relationship. We know this is not true from our experiences in other arenas. Many people are extraordinarily committed to their alma maters, for example, donating time and money to them years after graduation. Many people have similar relationships with former employers, particularly those where they held their first jobs. McKinsey & Company, for example, is famous for the level of commitment it enjoys from its former consultants—even those who were pushed out of the firm.

Indeed, short-term relationships often create a higher level of commitment than long-term relationships. One of the midterm exams given every year at Wharton asks members of the first-year class to explain how they were managed in their previous jobs. Almost without exception, the students coming from "terminal" jobs—those with fixed departure dates, such as junior analyst positions at investment banks—are the most positive about their former employers. The advantage of such temporary relationships is that the people in them have a clearer idea of what's expected of them and what they'll gain. They understand going in that they will have to work hard and that after a certain period they will have to leave. Not only are such employees committed to the companies during their tenure, but their positive feelings after they leave pay additional benefits to the companies—influencing word-of-mouth reputation, facilitating future business deals (why not deal with companies you know and like?), and creating a pool of potential future recruits.

Originally published in January–February 2000
Reprint R00101

Hiring Without Firing

CLAUDIO FERNÁNDEZ-ARAÓZ

Executive Summary

HIRING EXECUTIVES HAS always been a daunting task—and today's economy makes it tougher than ever. The global scope and breakneck pace of business, the shrinking supply of job candidates, and the constant shift of organizational structures have increased the stakes exponentially; one wrong hire can quickly derail a company. Yet recent studies indicate that between 30% and 50% of executive-level hires end in firings or resignations.

What makes hiring go wrong so often? And how can executives substantially improve the outcome of the process? This article provides some surprising answers to those questions.

Fernández-Aráoz presents ten common hiring traps and many real-world examples of how those traps have scuttled business plans in a variety of industries worldwide. A large consumer goods company, for instance, slipped into the *delegation gaffe* trap when it handed over the screening and interviewing process to a mismatched team of managers that had an agenda different from the CEO's. And the *ignoring emotional intelligence* trap tripped up a U.S. telecommunications company that hired a CEO with a great track record—only to fire him less than a year later when his lack of cross-cultural social skills was discovered.

Hiring well is a strategy—perhaps an organization's most important one, the author says. To sidestep the hiring traps, he suggests ways to systematically assess the company's needs and to determine how those needs mesh with the open job description—before candidates walk through the door. Fernández-Araóz's search strategy incites managers with hiring responsibilities to be creative, determined, and courageous when embarking on a candidate search.

HIRING HAS NEVER BEEN easy. About two thousand years ago, officials in the Han dynasty tried to make a science of the process by creating a long and detailed job description for civil servants. Archaeological records show that those same officials were frustrated by the results of their efforts; few new hires worked out as well as expected. Today business executives trying to fill senior-level positions carry on the unhappy tradition. Using interviews, reference checks, and sometimes even personality tests, they try to infuse logic and predictability into hiring. Still, success remains elusive. Several recent surveys conducted by both business academics and independent consulting firms have found that between 30% and 50% of all executive-level appointments end in firing or resignation.

If hiring has always been a daunting task, today's economy makes it more so. The global scope of business has increased the demand for talented senior executives in the corporate ranks. Meanwhile, supply is shrinking as more and more people—in particular, promising M.B.A.'s—choose to work for start-up ventures or go into business for themselves. At the same time, the nature of work itself is in flux. Until the 1990s, jobs were pretty uniform. In the classic, functional organization, everybody knew the responsibilities of the CEO and other senior executives. Most organizational cultures were relatively comparable, too—formal, hierarchical, and based on individual achievement. But with the advent of new organizational forms such as joint ventures and strategic alliances, and with the growing prevalence of teams, free agents, and networking, finding the right person to fill a job has become more complex. What competencies, after all, do these new kinds of companies and cultures require? Indeed, nowadays the CEOs of two companies in the exact same industry may need entirely different skills and personal styles to succeed.

For the past 13 years, I have conducted the searches of about 200 senior executives—most auspicious, some not—and have participated in the hiring of about one thousand more. As leader of professional development at Egon Zehnder International, I have learned about and discussed the prescient details of several thousand executive searches conducted by my colleagues around the world.

Our collective experience confirms what the Han officials discovered in 207 B.C.: it is impossible to turn hiring into a science. The process is often undermined by ten common mistakes, or "hiring traps." But we have also found that a systematic approach greatly improves the chances of hiring the right person. The approach, it should be said, requires time and discipline. But then, most matters of consequence do.

The Art of Hitting a Moving Target

Two recent cases illustrate the varied challenges of hiring in the new economy. The first case is well known—in fact, it was front-page news around the world. Last December, Franco Bernabè was hired to run Telecom Italia, a large, recently privatized conglomerate with a poorly performing stock price and a history of management turmoil. At the time, Bernabè appeared to be the perfect choice for the job: between 1992 and 1998, he had led the transformation of one of the world's largest energy companies, ENI, into a highly respected and profitable publicly traded business—and it, too, had a legacy of extreme senior-level upheaval. Bernabè's skills were considered so appropriate for his new position that Telecom Italia's stock rose 5% the day his appointment was announced—a multibillion dollar increase in market value.

Only two months later, Bernabè's job changed drastically when Telecom Italia became the target of a hostile takeover attempt by Olivetti Corporation. It became irrelevant, for instance, that Bernabè excelled at leading cultural change. To fend off Olivetti, he quickly needed to improve short-term financial results; rapidly assess the value and synergy of core and noncore business combinations; and almost instantly construct intricate investment and business obstacles that might thwart a takeover. In the end, it wasn't enough. Olivetti succeeded in its efforts, and Bernabè stepped down only six months after he started.

The second case also concerns a telecommunications company, this one based in the United States. It was seeking a CEO for its new division in Latin America. The division was not a start-up, per se, but a joint venture between two established local companies that had both been purchased by the U.S. business. As often happens, the former CEOs of the two acquired companies were appointed to the board of the joint venture and remained large shareholders. The board agreed that the new CEO would certainly need expertise in strategy formulation. The marketplace was getting crowded; it was now or never for entrants to establish their positions. And because the new venture had no marketing plan to speak of, the new CEO would also need expertise in high-tech sales and distribution. An international search was launched.

Three months later, the board hired an industry veteran who appeared to be tailor-made to run the new division. He had been extremely successful at the helm of a telecommunications company in the same sector, although in a different part of the world. He was an effective strategist—some said brilliant—and a proven marketing expert. He understood the company's technology, products, and customers far better than any of the other nine candidates.

But his run lasted less than a year and was nothing short of a disaster. The simple reason was that he lacked the two skills that the job really required: negotiation and cross-cultural sensitivity. This new CEO had to answer to three bosses with different agendas. The U.S. parent company wanted to use the new entity to push its own products and services in a new region. One former CEO-shareholder was more focused on the bottom line; he wanted to maximize profits by increasing prices. And the other former CEO-shareholder wanted to cut prices; volume was the key to success, he said. The new CEO was eager to make everyone happy—which turned him into everyone's enemy.

The bickering was exacerbated by cultural differences in communication styles. The Americans were confrontational. The Latin Americans were deferential, but only in public. Behind the scenes, their anger and frustration brought the company to a standstill. Senior executives, caught in the cross fire of warring bosses, started leaving the company in droves. Key distributors quickly picked up on the friction and abandoned the joint venture, seeking its products from other sources. By the time the CEO was fired, the company was close to bankruptcy.

Previous experience, once the "sacred cow" of successful hiring, can be meaningless.

But the next CEO had the company back on track—even thriving—within six months. While he had no experience in the telecommunications industry, the new CEO was a native of the Latin American country where the joint venture was based, and he was known and respected by its principals. He had also worked for ten years in the United States, which gave him special insight in understanding and dealing with the parent company's executives. His bridge-building skills quickly unified the new venture under one strategy.

Like the story of Franco Bernabè, this case illustrates the hazards of hiring in today's business environment. More and more, success depends on competencies that are intangible and rarely found on a person's résumé, such as flexibility and cross-cultural literacy. Previous experience, once the "sacred cow" of successful hiring, can be meaningless in an era when organizational forms are continually being invented and reinvented and job responsibilities sometimes change overnight. It's no wonder that a recent survey conducted by the International Association of Corporate and Professional Recruitment found that the main reason some external searches weren't completed, according to clients and consultants, was that the positions were either eliminated or redefined in the course of the searches.

Consider, too, the increased stakes of hiring today. When the economy moved at a less breakneck pace, mistakes could be more easily absorbed. Businesspeople— even high-level executives—could learn on the job. Indeed, with a few months to spare, the CEO of the new Latin American division might have learned to negotiate the cross-cultural minefield of conflicting agendas. But today, global competition, the capital markets, and the news media make a senior executive's performance a high-profile affair. It's hard to make an error, let alone try to recover from one, on stage.

The Ten Deadly Traps

Successful hiring is difficult—but not impossible. The right executives do sometimes end up in the right jobs. Otherwise organizations such as Sun Microsystems, Crédit Suisse First Boston, and international insurer AXA wouldn't be growing so effectively. It has been clear to outside observers that a systematic approach to key appointments has had a quantifiable effect on the successful expansion of those companies.

But we have found that hiring goes wrong as often as it goes right: Like other executive search firms, we are often called in because a high-level executive hiring has failed. Consider that in the last decade, the executive search business has experienced a 20% annual growth rate—much faster than the economy's growth rate.

So why does hiring go wrong so often? In most cases, the company has fallen into one—and often more—of the ten common hiring traps. None of the traps are the result of ill intentions; instead, they reflect many aspects of human nature and the pressing need for expedient solutions. Consider the following potential pitfalls:

THE REACTIVE APPROACH

Unless a company is entering a new market or is a startup, most job openings are the result of a firing or resignation. You might think that companies would start looking, then, for someone dramatically different from the departing executive—the rebound effect so common in second marriages. Instead, companies typically seek someone with the same good qualities of the previous jobholder but without the obvious defects. At an international shoe company, for instance, the director of distribution was fired because he constantly disagreed with peers, particularly the chief financial officer and the operations director. The company immediately began to look for someone who had the industry experience of the departed executive but who was "a good team player." And in fact, such a person was actually hired—then fired two years later because he never disagreed with anyone! What the company actually needed was an executive who was experienced in managing different channels and able to effectively convince his colleagues that the company's outdated distribution strategy needed to change.

The problem with the reactive approach is that it focuses the search on the familiar personality and effective competencies of the predecessor rather than on the job's requirements going forward. It also sets up the new hire for a lukewarm reception; no one can replicate his or her predecessor, and no one should be asked to.

UNREALISTIC SPECIFICATIONS

Time and time again, perfectly sensible search teams put together long and detailed job descriptions that could be filled only by Superman, Batman, and Spiderman—combined. In their bold exhaustiveness, these job descriptions are usually filled with contradictions: the candidate should be a forceful leader and a team player, a high-energy "doer" and a thoughtful analyst.

Such job descriptions are usually drawn up by a search team that interviews everyone in the company who will work with the new hire. The search team records each person's vision of the job's requirements and personal concept of what qualities lead to excellent performance. The specifications are usually compiled without considering the few critical priorities that the new manager should accomplish. Nor do they take into account which skills *already* exist in the organization.

The result of unrealistic specifications is that the universe of candidates becomes very small. And it may still leave out the best candidates who might have the essential mix of competencies needed for success even if they don't meet some of the specifications, such as an M.B.A. or a certain number of years of very specific experience.

EVALUATING PEOPLE IN ABSOLUTE TERMS

In business, praise and criticism are commonly doled out in absolute terms. It's said that Joe is a good manager or that Sally works hard. But such language can wreak havoc in the hiring process. After all, how can a search team intelligently assess a candidate's performance without a full understanding of the circumstances in which it was rendered? Joe might be a good manager of process but not of people. And Sally may work hard, but only when a promotion is in the offing.

Many job candidates don't tell the full truth, or at least they often finesse it.

During the interview process, executives often have a favorite set of questions that they ask regardless of the particulars of the situation. Two of the most common are: "What are your strengths and weaknesses?" and "Where do you want to be five years from now?" To the people asking them, these questions have good or bad answers— again in the absolute. The answers to absolute questions are opinions rendered in a vacuum and should be understood as such. The problem is, they are taken as fact.

ACCEPTING PEOPLE AT FACE VALUE

It is said that people are increasingly cynical and skeptical in these postmodern times, but you wouldn't know it from the typical hiring process. Candidates are almost always taken at face value. Executives readily believe their answers to interview questions and the information on their résumés. But many candidates don't tell the full truth, or at least they often finesse it.

The fact is many job candidates aren't thinking about long-term fit with a company; they're thinking about escaping a bad situation, or making more money, or hitching up with what appears to be a better organization. Résumés are edited to highlight successful experiences or to remove others entirely. And during interviews, people often "adjust" the truth to fit the question. For instance, an M.B.A. with three years of experience as a credit officer at a bank was extremely eager to be hired by a fast-growing technology company in Silicon Valley. When asked about his comfort with risk, the candidate spoke enthusiastically about how much he enjoyed loaning money to "gutsy little start-ups." In reality, he had loaned money to only two such ventures, and while the experience had been thrilling, the man's aversion to risk had also led him to reject about 150 other start-ups. Was his answer inaccurate? Technically, no. Was it the truth? Again, no.

The fact is, the hiring process isn't very conducive to complete candor. People want to put their best selves forward, and to do so often involves showing the camera your best angle. The problem is that most companies never try to see any other.

BELIEVING REFERENCES

Just as people tend to accept candidates at their word, so do they with references. But we have found that references, especially those provided by the candidate, are of extremely limited value. The reason: former (or current) bosses and colleagues are usually generous with their praise. They report the good, rarely the bad.

When selecting a potential employee, executives often think nothing of taking the word of a perfect stranger.

After all, they care far more about their relationship with the candidate than about helping a person they have never met make a good hiring decision. Some people may even be concerned about lawsuits. In fact, a recent survey of 854 executives conducted by the Society of Human Resource Management found that only 19% would reveal to reference-seekers why a candidate had left their company, and only 13% would describe a candidate's work habits. The reason: the executives said they feared being taken to court.

Interestingly, executives usually believe what they hear from a reference even when they don't know if that person is credible. There are few other circumstances in life in which we accept someone's judgment with such trust. Who would allow a surgeon to operate on them without hearing from several dependable sources that he was capable? We even turn to trusted friends and acquaintances when we pick a car dealer or a veterinarian. But when it comes to selecting a potential employee, executives very often think nothing of taking the word of a perfect stranger. Often, they feel as if they have no choice. Time is short. They also have no way of getting to know references well enough to judge their assessments. Executives trust strangers, they claim, because there is no alternative.

THE "JUST LIKE ME" BIAS

The full gamut of judgment errors comes into play in the hiring process. For instance, there's stereotyping—assuming that certain traits are associated with race, gender, or nationality. And there's the halo effect—letting one positive characteristic outshine all others. But the most pervasive bias of all is the tendency to highly rate people who are just like you. (When we praise people similar to ourselves, after all, we reinforce our own self-worth.) Thus, a Harvard M.B.A. who worked at a top consulting firm before he started his line-management experience will almost always prefer the candidate in the pack who has the same credentials. Unfortunately, sometimes the job would be better filled by someone with a different perspective or different skills.

DELEGATION GAFFES

Most executives want to make hiring decisions personally, and rightly so. They take it upon themselves to interview finalists and pick "the winner." However, many executives delegate the critical steps leading up to that point. Most often, they ask their direct reports or members of the human resources department to create the job description. Such delegation would not be bad if the people creating the description were properly briefed on the nature of the job opening and if top managers remained involved in the hiring process along the way. But that rarely happens; the executive is too busy. That's why he or she delegated the task in the first place.

Another delegation gaffe is that executives allow first-round interviews to be conducted by staffers who are either ill prepared for the evaluation or who don't have the right motivation. A large consumer goods company, for instance, was looking for a new country manager in Europe. It handed the job of reviewing résumés to a team composed of the six managers of the functional divisions. These individuals had mixed levels of experience in separating the wheat from the chaff. They also had their own opinions about what their new boss should be like—not all of which jibed with the job's demands or the CEO's standards. The company also asked the team to conduct the first round of interviews. That decision ended up losing the company one very promising candidate, who found the idea of being screened by her future subordinates downright insulting.

UNSTRUCTURED INTERVIEWS

Since World War I, extensive research has been conducted on the efficacy of various evaluation methods, including different forms of interviews, reference checks, personality tests, and even graphology and astrology. Without a doubt, the research has shown that *structured interviews* are the most reliable of all popular techniques for predicting performance.

The key word here is *structured*—meaning that the interviewer has a list of well-prepared questions designed to reveal the candidate's competencies—relevant knowledge, skills, and general abilities. Such interviews, which often include difficult or uncomfortable questions, must be carefully planned and executed. In reality, most interviews are anything but. They are loose conversations that cover subjects from the candidate's and the interviewer's mutual acquaintances to recent sports contests. When it comes to business, the interviewer lobs a few predictable questions to the candidate, who lobs them back. The session becomes a friendly chat. The participants may walk away from it happy, but little about the candidate's ability to perform has really been learned.

The costs of unstructured interviews are many, but perhaps the most damaging one is invisible: rejecting a highly qualified candidate who simply didn't excel at chitchat.

IGNORING EMOTIONAL INTELLIGENCE

So far, all the traps have reflected problems in how companies evaluate candidates. But there is another trap:

what companies look for—or rather, what they don't look for. Most companies look primarily, and even exclusively, at a candidate's hard data: education, IQ, job history, and the like. They rarely look at the soft data: the candidate's emotional intelligence. And yet, emotional intelligence is a critical predictor of professional success. According to research conducted by Daniel Goleman, author of the book *Working with Emotional Intelligence*, the components of emotional intelligence are twice as important for excellent performance as pure intellect and expertise. Goleman's research also found that for very senior leaders, close to 90% of success could be attributed to emotional intelligence competencies.

Egon Zehnder International conducted a study with more than 500 managers on three continents and found that unsuccessful managers had by far their largest deficiencies in emotional intelligence competencies. Their failure came despite significant strength in IQ and relevant experiences. That finding goes a long way toward explaining the old saw in the executive search profession, "Hired on experience, and fired on personality."

By now most people are familiar with the five components of emotional intelligence: self-awareness, self-regulation, motivation, empathy, and social skills. But familiarity with those traits doesn't make them easy to identify in others. Making matters harder still, every job requires different emotional competencies. One job—for instance, the CEO of a strategic alliance unit—might call for a surplus of the social skill commonly called conflict management. Another job—say a middle manager at a recently privatized company—might require a great deal of empathy and the specific competency of change catalyst. But most companies respond to the complexity of assessing emotional competencies by leaving them out of the hiring process entirely.

There is a final reason why companies don't measure emotional and social competencies, even when they know both are important. During the interview process, most people look like they have social competencies in spades. Indeed, people are trained throughout life to act cool, calm, and collected (not to mention friendly, collaborative, and kindhearted) when meeting people who will decide their fate.

POLITICAL PRESSURES

The last hiring trap is the most pervasive and daunting of them all. Indeed, well into my second decade in the executive search profession, the most spectacular hiring mistakes I have seen have been the result of well-meaning people who just happen to have agendas.

People, for instance, like to hire friends. Take the case of a forceful, dominating chairman who proposed that his college roommate succeed the company's fired CEO. Intimidated, the rest of the board agreed and waived the standard search and evaluation process. Within less than a year, the new CEO had to be fired; he lacked flexibility and strategic vision.

Some agendas are more Machiavellian. When joint ventures appoint senior executives, partners engage in all sorts of backstage scheming to get their candidates elected, hoping to have an ally in charge, regardless of skill. And in companies of all types, people routinely advocate for weak candidates so as not to diminish their own chances of getting ahead in the organization. In still other cases, candidates get jobs in return for favors rendered. For instance, a candidate might be hired with the anticipation that he will hire friends of his "supporters" or use the services of their companies. Such appointments, while common, can have a devastating effect not only on the company's performance but also on its morale.

Politics is so common (and pernicious) in hiring, perhaps it's not accurate to call it a trap. It's more like a pool of quicksand.

Getting Hiring Right

To avoid the ten hiring traps, executives must know what the pitfalls are—and how to sidestep them. But at the same time, it is essential to follow a systematic process with two major parts: *investing in the problem definition* and *doing the homework*. (On some occasions, professional help with hiring is advised. For a discussion of when such help is useful, see "Does Your Company Need Outside Hiring Help?" at the end of this article.)

Investing in the problem definition describes the work that a company should do before it even starts looking for candidates. Doing the homework describes the practices that make the evaluation process itself more insightful and, ultimately, more reliable and successful.

Let's start when an important job opens up. The company has a problem, but what is it? The easy answer could point the company toward one or more hiring traps—for example, the company determines that it needs to find a new executive who can do his predecessor's job, only better. But that reactive approach is bound to bring only incremental improvements to the job. The right answer requires a significant investment of both time and energy, with dividends to match. It suggests that the company define the current and future requirements of the position.

Without exception, those requirements will be driven by the company's strategy, and that's where the search team should begin. Is the organization trying to increase its market share? Does it plan to diversify? Is it seeking competitive advantage through cost or service? A generic assessment of the company's situation can also be useful when defining the problem. After all, turnarounds are well known to require certain types of managerial skills and personal aptitudes, such as rapid, accurate problem diagnosis, and comfort with uncertainty. Similarly, new business ventures often call for executives with high levels of initiative and innovation, and the ability to assemble and lead a winning team.

While overall company strategy and generic frameworks provide some initial orientation, every situation is unique. What really matters is a comprehensive understanding of the job opening itself. The executive who fills it will have priorities that can be determined—or at least opened up for discussion—by the following questions:

- Two years from now, how are we going to tell whether the new executive has been successful?

- What is it that we expect him to do, and how should he go about doing it in our organization?

- What initial objectives would we agree on?

- If we were to implement a short- and medium-term incentive system for this position, what key variables would matter most?

After generating a list of priorities, the search team needs to identify the position's "critical incidents," or commonly occurring situations that the new executive will confront and must be able to master to be considered a strong performer. Critical incidents can be culled by observing and interviewing effective managers in similar positions within the company, and by polling colleagues and employees of the incoming executive. They may also be gathered from the previous jobholder.

Critical incidents are often left out of the hiring process, perhaps because it takes time to develop a list of them. But they are enormously useful. For example, a consumer goods company that was hiring a new marketing manager asked five people in the organization to come up with three critical incidents. The new manager was certain to face sudden and unexpected price cuts by competitors and would have to know how to react swiftly. He would have to create new positioning for one product, overcoming the fact that its past positioning was well loved internally. And the new manager would have to recruit, develop, and retain high-potential product managers despite increased competition for those resources. By explicitly identifying these critical incidents, the company narrowed the focus of its search.

As a company delves into the problem-definition phase, a list of competencies for the job should be emerging. The new executive needs sound knowledge of certain technologies, for instance, or skill at motivating frontline workers. He needs strong analytical skills or a certain zest for risk taking. But don't fall into the trap of thinking that any single candidate will have every quality on the list. That's why it's useful to conduct an informal competency survey of the people who will be working closely with the new executive. They may have some of the desired competencies themselves, making those traits less than imperative in the new person. Key competencies that are entirely missing from the new executive's colleagues, or in short supply, should be explicitly identified—and moved to the top of the list.

One of the most successful hiring stories I have heard illustrates the importance and power of the above process. In 1990, a French executive was appointed to turn around a European conglomerate that had a bleeding bottom line and nine large business units that lacked competitive strategies. The CEO decided to replace every business unit head—and very quickly. In each case, he pinpointed the requirements of the open job and then looked for those competencies within the organization. When they were present in one person, he promoted that person to the top job. In other cases, he moved people with some of the necessary competencies to a lieutenant's position and hired an outsider with the "rest of the pieces" to the chief's job. With each hire, the CEO appointed unexpected individuals. None were champions in their industries, yet they brought the precise skills that were needed. The strategy has paid off; the conglomerate has created enormous shareholder value, uninterruptedly, for the last decade.

The problem-definition stage should also include a process to identify the job's requirements from a lateral point of view, or from the point of view of the new executive's would-be colleagues. Most job searches focus upward, on the boss's requirements, and downward, on the interests of the new person's direct reports. But in this day of teamwork, it is essential to bring to the surface the competencies, and even the personal traits, valued most by coworkers.

Of course, it is dangerous, if not impossible, to try to satisfy every constituency in an organization. But consider what happens when the concerns of colleagues are ignored, as so commonly happens. Several years ago, a leading European bank decided to launch a private banking business. A competent manager from one of the top U.S. private banks was hired as CEO and given full autonomy to build his team and open several branches. He did all this quickly and successfully, but the new manager had a propensity to deal cursorily with several of his peers and failed to develop effective and fair transfer pricing policies. He also failed to promote cross selling throughout the bank. Despite the executive's other successes, his trouble integrating with his colleagues caused such jealousy and resentment that the whole initiative had to be aborted after two years. That resulted in enormous financial and emotional costs.

By now in the problem-definition stage, a search team has generated a great deal of information about the open position and the person likely to make the most of it. It's time to create the final list of key competencies that will guide the search and evaluation effort.

For starters, every job description should state the minimum level of education and specific experience required. So many jobs are moving targets, but even if a job's requirements change overnight, a new hire with the minimum requirements would likely be able to manage in the short term. Long-term success, however, is determined by the heart of the job description: its list of key competencies. In general, there should be no more than six of these, or else you're in danger of creating unrealistic specifications. And in most cases, any competencies after number six can be supplied by the rest of the organization.

But what of the competencies themselves? How should they be worded? The simple answer is that competencies are useless unless they are described in behavioral terms. To illustrate this point, take the term "team player," which is often listed as a competency on job descriptions. But ask three people what team player means and you will get three different answers. For some, it means the ability to build group identity and commitment. To others, it means sharing the credit for work well done. Still others define a team player as someone who can draw all members into active and enthusiastic participation. Or consider "strategic vision,"

Every job description should include the emotional intelligence competencies critical to getting the work done.

another popular competency. To one executive, the term means the ability to conduct in-depth analyses of the forces at work in an industry. To another, it means the ability to inspire and guide people in a new direction.

Defining competencies in behavioral terms essentially imposes clarity. Take the case of a large industrial manufacturer that was looking for a general manager. The search team agreed that the new executive had to have the competency to be a "marketer." In most companies, that would do, but the search team went further, using the job description to translate "marketer" in the following way: "The candidate must be able to recognize an international business opportunity and create an environment that gets all the needed business units committed to the effort. He or she must be able to close the deal if needed, but to step away and recognize when to turn it over to a more qualified person closer to the deal."

No list of competencies would be complete without an acknowledgment of the personal and interpersonal factors required for success. Every job description should include those few emotional intelligence competencies critical to getting the work done.

Two years ago, a regional bank was looking for a new CEO who would have to oversee the forced merger of 11 smaller cooperatives. The search team immediately realized that the new CEO would need the competency of "conflict management." The job description wisely translated the term into behaviors as follows: "The ability to handle difficult people and tense situations with diplomacy and tact; spot potential conflict, bring disagreements into the open and help de-escalate them; encourage debate and open discussion; orchestrate win-win solutions." Today the bank is one of the most remarkable success stories in the country. The CEO who was hired, a master at conflict management, wasn't at that point a top expert in retail banking. But he put together an excellent team, with complementary skills, to achieve success.

A final and often quite tedious step closes the problem-definition phase: achieving consensus with all those involved in the hiring decision that the short list of competencies—and no other—will guide the search and evaluation process. At the very least, the new hire's boss should sign off on the list. Better yet, the boss, his boss, and any other key players in the process should, too. That might include members of the board, the head of human resources, and even some of the new hire's direct reports. That step can be tedious because it can involve a great deal of persuasion, which is both time consuming and energy draining. But like the rest of this phase, consensus is an investment that pays long-term dividends.

Doing the Homework

With a clear, agreed-upon list of competencies in hand, the next phase of successful hiring is generating and evaluating candidates and finally recruiting the right person.

What's the best strategy for generating a group of worthy people to consider? The first answer is something I call "high-leverage sourcing." In our experience, executives spend far too much time drumming up job candidates. They place advertisements, scan their Rolodexes or PalmPilots, and call friends and colleagues. It makes far more sense, however, to drum up people who are likely to know of several high-quality candidates at once. As you set out, don't look for the candidates themselves; look for people who know strong candidates.

Take the case of the CEO of a growing high-tech company in New York who was trying to hire a new head of sales. He placed an advertisement in the *Wall Street Journal* and scanned hundreds of résumés for almost three months, conducting about 20 interviews along the way. Still, no one filled the bill. Frustrated, the CEO finally ended up where he should have started: contacting knowledgeable people in his industry who could rattle off five or six candidates at a time. He spoke, for instance, to a former CEO at one of his suppliers who was now working at an industry consulting firm; that source supplied four viable candidates. He had lunch with a business school professor who advised several large companies like his own on distribution matters; that source yielded another five candidates. Not only did these sources understand the CEO's company and the job he was trying to fill but they had years of contacts. The CEO ended up hiring the one person who appeared on both sources' lists.

An open, creative attitude is, frankly, exceedingly rare among executives in the midst of hiring.

A second strategy for generating candidates involves adopting a "boundaryless mind-set." An open, creative attitude is, frankly, exceedingly rare among executives in the midst of the hiring process. The whole thing feels so difficult and risky to begin with, their gut tells them it is better to stick close to the rules. That's why most end up searching for people in similar industries or functions— or falling into the reactive approach and "Just Like Me" bias traps. Sometimes, executives focus only externally and don't give enough consideration to promising internal candidates. Conversely, some executives yield to convention or organizational pressures and look only inside when more promising prospects lay outside the company.

But successful searches throw off convention at the candidate-generating stage. For instance, when a European was appointed president of one of the largest foreign companies in Japan, he needed to orchestrate a quick turnaround of a deeply troubled organization. To fill a key spot, he immediately hired a director who had been fired by his predecessor. Many observers were shocked by such an unorthodox move, but the new president had chosen not to limit his options. Why not consider former employees?

Consider also the creativity of a hiring that has turned out, over the past few years, to be as successful as it was unconventional. The Central Bank of Argentina needed to hire a group of senior managers who would report directly to the bank's president and general manager. The situation was dire. The country was in the midst of a major reform to fight hyperinflation and restructure the economy. To avoid a potential crisis in the financial markets, the central bank needed to drastically strengthen its ability to properly control and advise the nation's major banks. The open jobs, then, would involve an enormous amount of responsibility and visibility—and they should have appealed to a large number of able professionals. But the public sector at that time had a very poor reputation as an employer. No one wanted to work for the government, especially not seasoned bankers.

Turning to industries outside banking, the search team decided that managers at top auditing firms working for the financial sector would also have the right qualifications. But how to lure them to the bank? The team knew that most of those firms had an "up or out" policy and that each year a portion of their qualified professionals weren't promoted. Why not approach those firms directly, the team asked itself, and explore the possibility of hiring—as a group—colleagues who could be on the way out anyway?

The plan worked. The auditing firms were eager to help the bank because they cared about the stability of the country's financial system. Many of the firms welcomed the search from the bank, and soon a group of managers was hired from one of the best firms in the country. Recruiting the group of managers for the central bank was made easier because the professionals knew they would be working with colleagues they trusted. And finally, the bank benefited enormously from the relationships the auditors already had with one another. The group was up and running literally within days—and it led the bank through its reform with flying colors.

Once a list of candidates has been generated, the evaluation phase begins. Sounds obvious enough, but companies usually combine evaluation with recruiting. In other words, they try to assess candidates at the same time as they try to sell them the job. That's a mistake. It diffuses the energy needed to fully and dispassionately evaluate candidates. Naturally, it's important to keep candidates interested in a possible job, but recruitment happens later in the process and shouldn't be allowed to muddy up the evaluation.

Instead, search teams should be focusing on conducting structured interviews. Conventional wisdom has it that the best interviewers are highly intuitive. That helps, but it is much more important to do the hard work of preparation. The best interviewers prepare a detailed plan for each meeting with a candidate—a plan that includes each competency to be investigated as well as the questions to measure each one. (For an example of such a plan, see "Beyond Conversation: The Hard Work of a Structured Interview.") Again, it is critical that questions focus on behaviors—and that they not be phrased in the absolute. It is meaningless to ask, "How do you feel about risk?" Better to ask, "What was a situation in which you faced risk, and how did you handle it?"

In the best-case scenario, structured interviews should be conducted by more than one person in the organization. In fact, the strategy of having several people evaluate candidates provides powerful checks and balances within the system—with one important caveat: multiple interviews are meaningful only if they are truly independent. The process doesn't work if one person interviews a candidate and then passes her along to the next interviewer with the message, "I think Nancy is great. Hope you like her, too." Interviews should be conducted in a vacuum of sorts. Each person should conduct his screening session without prior influence and should write up his impressions. Only later should those impressions be compared.

How many people should interview each candidate? Our experience suggests that a second evaluation reduces the possibility of hiring error from 50% to 10%, while a third evaluation practically guarantees a good decision.

The candidate should typically be interviewed by his boss, his boss's boss, and a senior human resources

Beyond Conversation: The Hard Work of a Structured Interview

Structured interviews are the result of careful planning and disciplined implementation. In fact, we have found that for a two-hour interview to yield meaningful information, it could take at least that much time to get ready for it. The most important part of preparation is creating a list of questions that will identify whether the candidate has the competencies required for the position. It means asking the candidate about his experiences and behavior, and yet most interviewers usually just let the candidate tell his story.

In a recent search for a marketing director for a fast-moving consumer goods company, we identified five competencies relevant to the position and a series of technical qualifications. Below are examples of some of the questions—focused on behaviors, not opinions or generalities—we used to measure each:

Competency	Questions Asked
Results oriented	• Have you been involved in a business or product launch? What were the specific steps you took to contribute to the success of the launch? • Describe the most successful marketing communications project you've led. How did you measure results?
Team-centered leadership	• Describe a time you led a team to be more effective. What did you do? How did the team and the organization benefit from your actions? • Describe a time you were asked to lead a particularly challenging team project. How did you overcome the obstacles you faced?
Strategic thinker	• What are the top three strategic issues that your current company faces? • Describe a situation in which you personally have been involved in addressing one of these issues. What actions did you take?
Change agent	• Describe a time when you received organizational resistance to an idea or project that you were responsible for implementing. How did you handle it? What resulted from it? Would you handle it any differently now? • Given our organizational culture and the changes we need, can you think of specific examples from your experience that would demonstrate that you would perform effectively and enjoy this position?
Ability to respond to deadline pressure	• Describe a time you made an extraordinary effort to meet a deadline? What were the results?

manager. It also makes sense to have the candidate interviewed by people in the company who are known to be experienced and insightful interviewers, regardless of their future relationship with the new executive.

Companies that rely on long-term employment as a competitive advantage should increase the number of interviews accordingly. At Egon Zehnder International, for instance, candidates are interviewed by up to 35 consultants in five countries; our annual turnover rate is 2%. But such extreme measures are hardly necessary in cases where the turnover rate isn't central to strategy.

Checking references is the next part of the systematic process of hiring without firing, and perhaps the most tricky. How, after all, do you overcome the superficiality built into the game? One answer is to speak with someone you know and trust who actually knows the candidate, if that is possible. The person may not be the candidate's boss or one of his colleagues, but perhaps they served together on a nonprofit board. Of course, you must also speak with the candidate's formal references, but make every effort to do so in person. Without a doubt, more information will flow at lunch than during a brief telephone call. It also gives you the chance to judge for yourself whether you trust its source.

The reference conversation should be characterized by the same rigorous preparation as the candidate's structured interview. Again, it means little to solicit general opinions about the candidate. Rather, describe the open job and its challenges. Has the candidate faced similar challenges in his current or past positions? How has he performed during them? The reference interview is also your main opportunity to probe for an accurate assessment of a candidate's emotional and social competencies. Remember that the candidates themselves are on their best behavior during interviews, making such competencies hard to judge firsthand.

Every job search, of course, finally ends—but not always as the search team would have hoped. Indeed, like a fish that wriggles off the hook as he is reeled in close to the boat, many of the best candidates get away when the focus of the hiring process shifts from evaluation to recruitment. The reason: the job is sold to them poorly, or not at all.

The most important part of selling a job is understanding the main motives—and the primary fears—of the candidate. Some people are motivated by money, others want challenge, and still others are eager to work with a great group of colleagues. A job offer needs to take such differences into account. It should even be tailored to do so. At the same time, it is critical never to promise something the company can't deliver. If a candidate seeks a great team but will be handed a mediocre one, say so. Nothing short-circuits a "successful" hiring faster than the new candidate walking into a lie.

As for fears, every person has a different attitude toward risk. In general, new hires that weren't looking for a new job—if they were recruited from the outset, for example—want their risk reduced. For instance, they don't want to be held responsible for first-quarter results if they are coming into the organization too late to affect them. Others may be concerned about a potential spin-off of the business, or if the company is family owned, about the role of family members in day-to-day operations. Some of those risks can easily be "insured" through contractual conditions. Clarity always facilitates a smooth integration.

Finally, nothing convinces more than conviction. If you want a candidate, go out of your way. Some of the best hires I have witnessed have been the result of an outstanding level of persistence. The CEO of a major oil company, for example, pursued the ideal chief operating officer candidate for six months. He had countless meetings with him and even with his family—including a celebration with both families on New Year's Eve. Even after the candidate accepted the job, and then rejected it the next week, the CEO persisted with meetings, notes, and phone calls. Finally, the man took the job and has performed even better than was hoped.

The Courage to Hire Wisely

Hiring well requires a systematic approach. But just as important, it requires discipline—and perhaps even that is not a strong enough word. It takes courage. Given the pressures of time and convention—not to mention organizational politics—it is easy to fall into any number of traps.

To keep hiring on the high road, executives must never veer from the agreed-upon list of competencies, otherwise the process is almost instantly corrupted. They must invest the time and effort to define the problem and do the homework; there are no shortcuts to the information these steps generate. And finally, executives must instill the discipline of the process in others. After all, no executive can implement a strategy alone. And hiring well is just that—a strategy. It may, in fact, be the organization's most important one.

Countless times, I have seen a systematic approach fall apart when expediency gets in the way. In one case, an influential board member suddenly demanded the job description be rewritten to better reflect the skills of his top choice. In another, the finalist received a terrible reference in the eleventh hour. Both times, momentum took over. The job description was changed and the board member's candidate was hired. The terrible reference was ignored and the finalist got the job. Courage would have meant difficult conversations and even confrontation, but perhaps both stories would have had happier endings. Of course, both new hires were eventually fired.

Does Your Company Need Outside Hiring Help?

IN MANY ORGANIZATIONS, whether to use outside hiring help is a perennial, and often controversial, question when a senior-level job opens. It's controversial because executive search firms can be expensive. The professional fees for the search of a senior executive can easily amount to several hundred thousand dollars. And while that amount can be negligible compared with the costs of failure or the benefits of a smart hire, people still wonder whether external help will actually improve the hiring decision at all.

They may have a point. As a partner of an executive search firm, I know there are times when professional help is unnecessary.

One example is when the pool of candidates for a job is small and well known, and the specific need is very straightforward. Take the case of a Washington-based think tank that was looking for an analyst of global economic trends. The organization had two very talented internal candidates for the job, and its board members were personally acquainted with the dozen-or-so external candidates—all of them scholars or members of other think tanks. The chairman also had a very clear view of what was needed. Indeed, one of the internal candidates was quickly and successfully promoted.

Outside help also doesn't make sense when a company is conducting a search for the umpteenth time—that is, it knows well the requirements of an open job and the competencies of the person who will best fill it. External help is probably not a wise investment for some highly technical positions, where very specialized know-how and expertise are key. Those "hard" competencies are easier to evaluate than "soft" managerial and leadership abilities and don't call for experts. Finally, the lower the level of the position, the lower the value of external help. In such cases, it just doesn't pay.

But several situations present a strong case for calling in a professional search firm.

The first is when a company is hiring for very high-level positions that have great impact on the bottom line. Even if an executive search firm finds a candidate who generates only 1% more profits than an alternative candidate does, it has paid for itself many times over. Moreover, professional firms are often better than in-house staff at conducting the fast and confidential searches often required in high-level situations.

Outside help also makes sense in the case of new jobs created by diversification, new markets, or joint ventures. In such situations, an organization might not be familiar with the key competencies required for the open spot and will have a limited knowledge of potential candidates and how to evaluate them.

Professional firms can also add value when a company wants to cast its net particularly wide in its search for a new executive. For example, an investment company with a reputation for stodginess decided to look for a new marketing director in what to the investment firm was the "mysterious" world of consumer product branding. Because of its accumulated experience, the search firm it retained generated a list of excellent candidates from the automobile, breakfast cereal, and clothing industries. The company ended up hiring the breakfast cereal marketing executive, who did indeed rejuvenate the company's brand.

Finally, an executive search firm is advised if a company needs help recruiting a much sought after candidate. The reason: many search firms have rich experience crafting the complex job contracts that such candidates require. They know how to creatively build in incentives and bonuses and minimize a candidate's perceived risks. In this day of newfangled financial instruments—stock options, exploding offers, and so on—it can pay to call in professionals.

As in any outsourcing arrangement, a company that opts to use an executive search firm should proceed with caution. After all, hiring a senior manager is a strategic decision. A company's executives must stay involved every step of the way. Here's how:

Select a consultant, not just a firm

Picking a search firm based only on its literature is like hiring an executive based only on his résumé. In selecting a search firm, conduct multiple interviews with the firm's consultant and check references with some of its clients. Make sure you ask about the stability of the firm's professional staff and the mechanisms it uses to enhance collaboration. Firms with stable staffs who share their knowledge are more likely to have built a unique store of information about potential candidates and how to evaluate them effectively.

Like many professional service firms, some executive search firms use seasoned partners to land assignments, and they use less experienced people, including newly minted M.B.A.'s, to conduct the searches. So make sure your selection process includes meeting the consultants who will actually be handling each step of your search. You will want to assess their experience and technical competence and get a read on their availability, affability, and candor.

Avoid potential conflicts

Because so many search firms are paid at least partly on commission, they are likely to promote an external candidate—even when an internal candidate is equally qualified. Similarly, when search firms are paid a percentage of a new hire's compensation package, they might be motivated to look for expensive candidates or negotiate overly rich contracts. A flat fee or retainer arrangement helps avoid all those problems. In fact, I would worry about any firm that does not offer such options.

Work as a team

An effective search is the result of a partnership between search firm and client. Your full involvement is critical, starting with the problem definition, through the homework stage, and into the final offer. While consultants can add value throughout this process, nobody knows the job and the organization better than its own executives.

Originally published in July–August 1999
Reprint 99403

Making Partner

A Mentor's Guide to the Psychological Journey

HERMINIA IBARRA

Executive Summary

FOR YEARS, PARTNERS AT professional service firms considered the leap from professional to partner a function of "natural selection"—a test of survival of the fittest. But that model is on the verge of extinction: in today's firms, securing and retaining talent is becoming paramount as young MBAs, once willing to log years of hard labor in hopes of being made partner, are leaving in hordes for hot new Internet companies.

So how can companies keep the talent they've worked so hard to cultivate? One way, Ibarra says, is to have partners take a more active mentoring role in helping junior professionals create a partner persona. She explains the three steps that senior colleagues can take to guide junior professionals on this journey.

The first has to do with observing role models. By taking a *collage* approach, young professionals can survey a broad range of personalities and so accumulate a larger repertoire of possible styles to choose from. For their part, partners can assist in this observation process by communicating explicitly what styles work for them and why. The second step partners can take is to encourage professionals to develop a repertoire of role models; by working with many senior professionals, junior colleagues are more apt to find just the right mix of mentors. And third, senior people can take extra care to support young professionals at the most difficult moments in the process.

Indeed, the leap from professional to partner is difficult—even trying at times. But for those willing and daring enough to take the leap—and for those who've already made it—understanding the associated psychological and emotional obstacles is critical to success.

At some point in their careers, every management consultant, investment banker, and accountant must attempt the leap from professional to partner. For some, it's an easy jump over the crevasse. They have learned what it takes to woo clients and keep them satisfied; they have learned to lead with confidence. But for most, it's a frustrating and confusing experience in which they arrive at the other side of the crevasse bruised and battered. Still others fail in the attempt and ultimately leave the firm broken.

For years, partners at professional service firms considered the leap a matter of natural selection—an entirely acceptable test of survival of the fittest. They reasoned that they had made it over the crevasse themselves; those who couldn't—well, they didn't have the right stuff for the firm anyway. But the war for talent currently raging in these booming economic times has changed that kind of thinking at many firms. Talented MBAs, once willing to log as many as ten years of hard labor in hopes of being made partner, are now getting increasingly hard to find—let alone keep. They're leaving in hordes for hot new Internet companies. Now, even prestigious firms like McKinsey & Company and Goldman Sachs find themselves buying talent in a seller's market.

The bottom line is that professional service firms can no longer afford to let natural selection take its course. To keep their senior ranks full, they must help the professionals whom they have cultivated and led to the brink cross over it. But how? The answer is not to lower the standards for making partner. Rather, partners must actively mentor their young colleagues, tutoring them on how to make—and survive—the leap. To do so, they must acknowledge and become involved in a transformation process they understand in their bones but rarely discuss out loud: helping aspiring partners forge a new identity.

Unfortunately, aspiring partners are in a catch-22: They are expected to act like partners before they have the competencies and client relationships—in short, the credibility—to actually do so. They are also in the difficult position of having to change their view of themselves—where they fit in with the firm and how they can contribute. They must speak and act with confidence as representatives of their firms and as peer advisers to more senior, experienced

There are few professional transformations quite as psychologically complex as the transformation to partner.

managers. In short, they must assume a new and different professional identity, a change that can be a wrenching, self-questioning experience.

It is an experience made worse by the fact that most junior professionals take the leap to senior roles without much formal guidance from their organization. They fly solo. They improvise. For most, therefore, the transition process feels random and erratic, and the criteria by which they are judged, amorphous. Unguided, some take wild stabs at what they think acting like a partner entails. Others take an inordinately long time to discover what it takes to become truly effective. Frustrated, they may eventually assume they are just not right for the job and seek other employment opportunities. Many firms have lost precious talent in just this way.

Of course, some professionals stick with it, and most of them ultimately develop a new but genuine identity as a partner. But even for those individuals, the journey is still trying, for in the midst of it, most individuals question their authenticity. They struggle with the "fake it till you make it" approach they feel obliged to adopt as a stopgap measure. They struggle with issues of integrity. Indeed, there are few professional transformations quite as psychologically complex as the transformation to partner.

Some young professionals enjoy rich apprenticeship experiences along the way, but that is rare, now more than ever.

In recent years, I have studied 35 aspiring partners at several large professional services firms (assisted by research assistants Jennifer Suesse and Naomi Atkins of Harvard Business School). I discovered that those individuals who successfully advanced used a distinct approach to observing role models, experimenting with new behaviors, and evaluating their progress. Those who advanced less quickly and effectively used a different approach—one with markedly less flexibility and risk. To be successful mentors, partners need to be aware of both approaches and know how to guide and support aspiring partners toward the more effective one.

A New Mentoring Landscape

Not every young professional is left to fend for himself on the road to becoming partner. Some enjoy rich apprenticeship experiences along the way, but that is rare, now more than ever. Today, most partners are out chasing business themselves; in this fiercely competitive and opportunity-laden economy, they have to. Thus, young professionals seeking to make the leap are often left with snippets of vague advice, the most common being: "If you want to be a partner, start acting like one." Worse, many professionals often receive two contradictory pieces of counsel: "Just act like I do" and "Just be yourself."

Technically speaking, none of these shreds of counsel is wrong; they are all just maddeningly unhelpful. Certainly, partners know more, but usually their insights are the kind of tacit knowledge that can be hard to express in words. Perhaps that is why, when pressed for additional advice, they offer vague suggestions such as "Keep working on your confidence" or "Try to improve your presence." True, becoming a partner requires a professional to change not only her skills but also her communication style. But the transition requires a deeper, personal transformation, too. And it is here, in the creation of an identity, where aspiring partners flounder and need the most help.

Consider the case of a professional in my study who was known in his consulting firm as an excellent analyst. After five years of grueling assignments with clients around the world, it was time for him to "grow or go," as he was told. "To be really successful at this game, I need to let go of the image I have of myself as the one who knows all the facts. Instead, I have to think of myself as, and be perceived as, the adviser to the client," he said at the time. "But it's just such a different role for me. It's like my whole basis for existence is cut away if I can't rely on the data."

This consultant felt panicked, but he ultimately continued to advance quite well along the road to partner. Like others in my study who made their way up the ranks, he used a strategy that initially seemed erratic, but upon closer examination proved to be a three-part iterative learning process of observing role models, experimenting with new behaviors, and evaluating the results of those experiments.

To illustrate this process, let's consider two other professionals: Robert Foreman, a 29-year-old consultant, and Liz Brenner, a 27-year-old investment banker. A look at their different approaches to the same basic strategy will highlight the more effective one. (Both Foreman and Brenner represent participants in my study; their names, like all others in this article, are fictitious.)

For six years, Robert Foreman was known as a stellar associate—great with numbers and capable of solid market analysis. But as the time for being named partner approached, he was told he needed to improve his presence with clients. Immediately, Foreman set about searching for role models. His first choice was his boss, a partner named Joe McDuffy, whose personality was diametrically opposed to Foreman's own laid-back style. As

Foreman described McDuffy: "He is very direct about what he thinks needs to be done. He'll even tell clients bluntly that they're wrong."

Foreman tried to emulate McDuffy but quickly found out that he could not adopt that style. At one meeting, for instance, Foreman overcompensated by being arrogant with a client, which backfired. He decided to stick closer to his own style and search for other models. In doing so, he discovered that the partners' styles could be arrayed on a continuum from aggressive to exploratory. As he explained, "Both ends of the spectrum work, but the majority are on the aggressive end. McDuffy, Lewis, Roberts, Foxworth, and Richardson, for example, are all very directive and driving with clients. Madden defines the other end of the continuum. He's the exploratory, 'let me take you on a journey' type."

In meetings over the next few months, Foreman took every opportunity to try different behaviors, which he learned from closely watching a variety of people: "Richardson was useful on how to have the guts to confront senior people," he recalled, "and McDuffy gave me some pointers about focusing clients on the critical issues. I watched how Madden manages one-on-one client interactions." By mixing some of their behaviors with his own style and trying them in client meetings, Foreman started to feel better about expanding his repertoire. For example, he combined McDuffy's direct approach with his own more laid-back style: he told clients when he thought they were wrong but softened his words so as not to offend them.

As he experimented with a variety of behaviors, Foreman noticed that his senior colleagues were giving him constructive tips more frequently. One partner even asked him to run a series of meetings in her absence.

Foreman's clients also seemed to respond favorably; they asked his opinion more and more and often recalled particularly salient points he had made in previous meetings. Within six months, Foreman said, "Not only have I figured out how to be good at this, but I've figured out how to do it without really compromising who I am." He had created a new identity by being true to himself and by emulating others.

Liz Brenner also had a reputation as an excellent associate, with particularly strong skills in technical analysis and time management. But during her third-year review, Brenner was told that she should be taking a more active role in client meetings. The advice did not surprise her; she knew she tended to be shy in client situations. "With the people at my firm, I'm argumentative, rigorous, and demanding," she said. "But when I'm with clients, I become careful; I'm less inclined to give my own opinion. That's why I have trouble getting new clients to focus on the issues and establishing a presence right from the start."

Brenner knew instinctively that senior executives in the firm could show her what it took to become a partner. But the problem was that she just couldn't find an appealing role model. Since joining the firm, she had worked with Daniel Morris, a managing director, on almost every deal. But she didn't like his style, which she considered abrupt and arrogant. "Daniel is successful," she noted, "but I don't respect him as an individual."

Brenner had also worked closely with Brian Finn, another director, whom she admired a great deal for his friendly approach. But again, she felt she couldn't use him as a model. "Finn is extremely laid-back with clients, almost not asking for the business. But it wouldn't work for me. It only works for Finn because he already has the years of experience behind him," she explained.

Unable to find someone to emulate, Brenner decided to work with what she had. She knew that her strengths lay in her analytical skills and therefore focused on how best to display those skills with clients. Prior to meetings, she spent hours researching the client's industry from every possible angle. She walked into meetings with better-designed charts and more comprehensive reports than usual. Unfortunately, in several cases, the client's questions were not the ones she had prepared for, so she remained in her usual supporting role.

For 12 months, Brenner struggled with how to present herself to clients. Before each new client meeting, she pored over data and analyses. She even took courses on how to make better presentations. Over time, Brenner found that most of her clients came to trust her knowledge and expertise. But in the meantime, as her formal evaluations pointed out, she was unable to grab clients' trust and attention from day one. Although she felt good about maintaining her integrity, she noticed that she wasn't receiving as many pointers from her senior colleagues as she had

Creating a partner persona involves three tasks: observing role models, experimenting with possible selves, and evaluating their results.

when she first started with the firm. And she didn't seem to be getting repeat business in the way that some of her more aggressive counterparts were. Brenner often felt that she just wasn't cut out to be an investment banker, since it required her to forgo her natural style. "I'm just not one of those people who loves talking about things they know nothing about," she said.

As time went on, Brenner continued to focus on the "substantive" style she had cultivated. But she gradually came to rely a little less strictly on data analysis. In preparation for client meetings, she started to spend more time with senior colleagues who understood the particular intricacies of the client's field. But she continued to feel uncomfortable in client situations. By the end of my study, Brenner was still in the running for partner, but she was progressing much more slowly and was certainly enjoying the process less than Foreman.

Observing Different Styles

As I've said, creating a partner persona involves three tasks: observing role models, experimenting with possible selves, and evaluating their results. Foreman and Brenner do all three, but they are a study in contrasts. Take their approaches to observing and selecting role models. Foreman discerned the wide variety of behaviors available for emulation, especially after his first attempts to imitate McDuffy failed. In watching his seniors, he was asking himself, "Is there only one right way to do this? What are my options for being effective? For signaling my professionalism?" Through unrelenting observation, he came up with a medley of effective behaviors, including being directive, driving, and soft-spoken.

Similarly, Brenner noticed that both arrogant and friendly styles could be effective in dealing with clients. She, too, observed that there was more than one way to act like a partner. But understanding the spectrum of possibilities is just part of the observation process. Professionals must also decide which behaviors to actually emulate from the choices before them. They must hold each effective behavior up to themselves and evaluate it, asking, "Does this resonate with who I am? Will it work for me? Do I want to be like this person?"

Foreman compared the styles he observed to his sense of self: "I can be like this, but I don't like it," and "He's the exploratory type. . . . This is where I see myself." I call this process *identity matching*. There are two dynamics at work here: the feasibility of the behavior— "Will it work for me?"—and its appeal—"Do I want to do this?" Ultimately, Foreman located a role model whose quieter approach he found effective and appealing. He later found several examples of other behaviors that were also feasible, such as focusing clients on critical issues and pushing back when he knew a client was wrong.

While Brenner observed a similar panoply of behaviors, she wasn't as successful as Foreman in finding an identity match. She knew she could be arrogant like her first model, but she did not find the style appealing. And while she found the friendly style of her second senior partner more appealing, she thought it less effective for her because of her age and inexperience.

It's easy to attribute Brenner's subpar results to her selection of poor role models and to her pickiness. But there's more to it. Foreman observed several role models simultaneously; Brenner focused her attention on one senior colleague at a time. Foreman learned from each of his models: he saw senior partners in terms of their specific strengths and traits. Then he was able to customize those behaviors to his needs and preferences. Even though he didn't identify entirely with the "aggressive" Richardson, for example, he observed a particular style of his—a willingness to confront clients when he believed them to be wrong—that he wanted to model. Brenner, by contrast, viewed role models more monolithically. She saw everything the partners represented—their personal style and professional values—as a package deal and made a value judgment based on that package. Her approach was all or nothing.

Foreman and Brenner exemplify, respectively, what I term *collage* and *holistic* approaches to observation.[1] Like Foreman and Brenner, most young professionals start out with a holistic approach, because in their early careers they are assigned to and work closely with only one person. As they encounter a greater number of senior colleagues, many, like Foreman, begin to take a collage approach. But others do not. That's too bad, because the collage approach is clearly more effective. The reason is simple: by observing a broad range of personalities and picking out specific behaviors, collage observers can accumulate a larger repertoire of possible styles to choose from—and do so more quickly—than the holistic observers.

Psychologist Hazel Markus coined the phrase "possible selves" to illustrate the range of identities a person can have.[2] Because they see more possible selves, collage observers are more likely to find behaviors that fit who they are, who they want to be, and what they can do. That becomes especially helpful as professionals begin to move from observation to experimentation.

Testing, and Testing Again

As one participant in my study summarized, "Forty percent is watching what the partners do. Sixty percent is mustering the courage to try it yourself." Eventually, every aspiring partner must act—and that means experimenting. Once again, Foreman and Brenner illustrate contrasting approaches.

Understanding that his new role as client adviser required different behavior, Foreman actively sought to find a model whose style was the antithesis of his own. He was, in fact, so eager to depart from his comfort zone of natural behaviors that he actually overcompensated and annoyed the client. When this experimental aggressive self failed, he took every available opportunity to try out other behaviors he had gathered in his collection. Foreman's approach is what I call the *chameleon strategy*.

Brenner, by contrast, didn't want to change herself to fit the situation and therefore refused to experiment with behaviors that felt unnatural to her. She used what I call the *true-to-self strategy*. Indeed, even though she knew that the situation required a more aggressive persona, she remained faithful to the behaviors that had worked for her in the past. Unlike Foreman, she practiced her own substantive style over and over again.

Brenner was reluctant to experiment with vastly different behaviors in part because she doubted her ability to add value to the conversation. But she was reluctant also because she viewed herself as more authentic than senior partners like Morris, whom she saw as insincere and manipulative. Each experiment was therefore guided not by what she had observed in more experienced senior partners but by her sense of self. Unfortunately, her substantive style was inappropriate for her new role, so as she sought to perfect it, all she did was spin her wheels. Her attempt to protect her authenticity thwarted her learning process.

Evaluating from All Sides

For chameleons and true-to-selves alike, the experimentation stage of the learning process is emotional and difficult. But their struggles in this endeavor would be in vain without some means of evaluating the behaviors they'd tried. Aspiring partners must analyze what worked and what didn't and view each new experiment as bringing them one step closer to reaching their goal. Over time, most juniors refine and perfect their approach, honing in on a style that is both effective and authentic—but this takes time. The speed and outcome of this process depend on the quality of self-reflection and the quality of feedback that junior people receive from their more experienced colleagues.

Most young professionals in my study said they evaluated their behavior experiments by performing a sort of internal litmus test. They compared their actions to their sense of self, essentially asking "Was I true to myself? Did I behave in ways that are congruent with who I am and who I want to be?" Brenner couldn't bring herself to imitate others because it just didn't feel right. Foreman felt his experiment with an aggressive style failed because he found it to be "depressing" and at odds with his concept of an "ideal self." Without a sense of self-congruence, new behaviors are less likely to be retained and practiced. The discomfort Foreman felt from his experiment taught him a great deal about how he might gradually adapt his behaviors to accomplish the same goals. He went back to the drawing board to design a new experimental behavior, this time based on his natural style. As he continued his experiments, he honed behaviors that were increasingly congruent with his sense of an ideal self and sought role models whom he felt were better matches.

As Foreman's actions show, the chameleon's propensity for trying out different behaviors generates more variety in his experiments. This leads to greater self-discovery and a greater chance that he will figure out what works for him. The true-to-self person will refuse to try a different behavior on the grounds that it might not feel right. Chameleons know for certain whether or not a behavior departs too much from who they are and want to be because they have tried it. After trying behaviors different from their own, the chameleons in my study reported that they often

Because they tend to progress faster, chameleons are seen as "moving in the right direction." They will inevitably get more pointers from senior partners.

caught themselves thinking, "That wasn't so bad!" and "I can do this!" Their reactions were experience-based rather than imagined or hypothesized.

In the end, junior professionals need to ask themselves, "Was I credible? Was I competent? How did my clients, superiors, and colleagues judge my performance?" They need to look to clients and senior colleagues to discover whether their experimental styles are effective. Foreman, for instance, knew that some of his experimental behaviors were working because his clients began to rely on him and call him more. But while Foreman's earlier experiment failed by his own standards, Brenner's trial failed because it simply did not meet her client's standards.

Indeed, clients and senior colleagues react differently to chameleons than they do to true-to-self people. Because they tend to progress faster, chameleons are seen as "moving in the right direction." And because senior partners are often more willing to help out someone they see as a rising star, the chameleons will inevitably get more pointers from them. Many, like Foreman, also receive opportunities to lead meetings and so forth—opportunities they wouldn't have had otherwise.

True-to-selves, by contrast, are perceived as "not getting it." Partners gradually spend less time giving them feedback, and they are essentially left to figure things out on their own, as Liz Brenner was.

No matter which experimentation approach juniors choose, their internal and external evaluations will help them make the necessary corrective adjustments to their strategies. An assessment of their experimental behaviors will lead them to a mature, experienced-based understanding of what the role entails. It will also help reduce the discrepancy between their view of themselves and the behaviors that are required to perform their job successfully.

As Brenner and Foreman's experiences show, the learning process that underlies forging a new identity is full of loops and discoveries. Figuring out what to learn, whom to learn from, and how to act is not easy. No one gets it right on the first try. Each step of the process may send the junior in a different direction—to different models or different behaviors. But as they cycle through the process, juniors will, like Foreman, figure out how to be good at what they do without compromising who they really are.

Throwing a Lifeline

Parents who understand—and empathize with—the traumas of adolescence are often in a better position to help their children through that stage in their lives. The same can be said for the partners in professional service firms who are sympathetic to junior colleagues trying to forge a new identity. Partners who understand that young professionals are in the process of observing, experimenting with, and evaluating various personas can guide and support them throughout the transition. Here's how.

Communicate explicitly what works for you and why. Among the most striking findings in my study were the different conclusions professionals drew from watching the same senior people. Those who watched partners from a distance often interpreted their success with cynicism: "He only tells the clients what they want to hear," "His technical skills aren't great; he's just a great schmoozer." But professionals who watched partners up close, and heard those partners' own insights about their approach to business, formulated much more positive views: "She doesn't raise defensive feelings in clients yet is able to get her point across," "He may not be our most brilliant banker, but he's great with clients because he makes them feel valued."

In most cases, giving pointers did not constitute a significant drain on the senior person's time: a strategy conversation a few minutes before walking into a meeting (such as, "Watch how I sequence who I call on in the discussion"), or a quick debrief on the plane returning from an engagement. These are the moments that unveil the mysteries for the junior professional. They are also moments that allow the junior person to view the senior as someone they would like to emulate. In explaining themselves to junior colleagues, partners help expand the professional's repertoire of possible selves.

But senior people would do well to go beyond on-the-fly explanations of their behaviors and offer their junior colleagues a robust, comprehensive point of view on the craft of being a partner. This perspective might also include a partner's analysis of the business in general—its opportunities and challenges, its key players and its future. Indeed, at one firm I studied, the most successful junior professionals repeatedly mentioned how much they were helped by a partner who took the time to tell them stories about the business and how to succeed as a partner. His well-articulated philosophy contained the following advice, which is notable for its gritty explicitness:

> *As a junior team leader, when the client says "We want you to do X," you say, "Great." As you get more senior, you're more likely to say, "Let's talk about X." You try to identify where the real problem is. For example, a client might ask us to help them figure out if they should close a plant in France. Your job is to try to understand the business, their basis for making money. You might end up saying to them, "Your problem is not in manufacturing. What's going to be key to your success is your brand image." It's about taking the big-picture perspective and understanding how things fit into the client's overall strategy.*

Many professionals who worked with this partner referred to him as a great teacher who helped them make sense of the mysterious process in which they were immersed.

Encourage professionals to develop a repertoire of role models. Partners can also help their junior colleagues find the right mix of role models—a task that is more complicated than it sounds. As one person in my study recalled, "My boss stopped by my office and said it was time for me to get some role models. Then he threw out the names of three women in the industry. They were the usual suspects—high powered, successful. They all acted pretty much the same, and I knew I wasn't like that." In other words, partners need to take a junior professional's own style into account when suggesting role models. Partners must also recognize that suggesting a wide variety of "types" can be extraordinarily useful.

Mentors can also play a critical role in the transition by helping their protégés devise explicit criteria on which to judge potential role models. As I've already noted, juniors should ask themselves three questions at the observation stage: "Is the role model successful?" (effectiveness); "Would her behavior work for me?" (feasibility); "Is her persona appealing to me, and do I want to be like her?" (attractiveness). Keeping those questions in mind, mentors can suggest people who might round out the junior's portfolio of role models. To do this, they should pay attention not just to the skills the junior needs to develop but also to what kinds of issues they might struggle with while trying to define who they want to become. Partners can suggest how juniors might combine a favorite role model's demeanor with the skill set of another mentor. They can also help the junior person see beyond the surface elements of style; perhaps they cannot adopt the same style their favorite model uses to make a first impression, but they may be able to learn a great deal from the strategy behind those tactics.

Provide emotional and practical support to professionals at the most difficult moments. At some point, every aspiring partner needs to be nudged to stop observing and start experimenting. A senior executive can help by bringing this point out into the open, essentially telling junior professionals, "You cannot avoid experiential learning." Informed of the emotional tenure of the learning process, seniors can also frame experimentation as a series of "small probes" to help aspiring partners discover the mature professional they will become rather than exercises in being an impostor.

Partners can also help professionals find low-risk ways to learn about possible selves. For example, they can encourage a junior person to practice new behaviors in internal meetings before trying them with clients. Partners can also help junior colleagues secure new clients with whom they have a better chance of establishing a peer relationship. It is often difficult to negotiate a new role or identity in a long-standing relationship. Old clients are accustomed to the junior professional's old persona. Therefore, if partners set their junior colleagues up with new relationships, they create an environment more conducive to active experimentation.

Finally, for those juniors who really resist taking the leap, seniors can help them recognize that the just-be-yourself strategy may slow their progress. In many cases, this true-to-self approach may simply be a defense mechanism for avoiding possible failure. Indeed, the best advice a partner can give is, "Stop being yourself—but don't worry, everyone must go through this phase. It's called learning."

The Organizational Challenge

Partners can play an active role in mentoring their young colleagues, but they should not go it alone. Organizations—in the form of the HR department or senior leadership team—can also play a role in helping aspiring partners take the leap successfully.

The first frontier is the assignments process. Traditionally, professional service firms have used the assignments process to expand the technical skills and industry expertise of their junior people. In some firms, individuals are encouraged to stick with the same partner for many years, especially when the chemistry is good. The argument for this apprenticeship model is that it allows the professional to learn in-depth from one master. But even if a partner and professional "click" on this level, there is still much to be gained by using the assignments process to expand a professional's exposure to other role models. In other words, professional service firms need to think creatively about whom professionals should learn from and not just what they should learn.

The assignments process is also critical in helping slow starters initiate the leap. The reason? Young professionals often play to expectations. Their partners and peers expect them to act a certain way, and so they are reluctant to take on a new persona publicly. But a new assignment can get an aspiring partner in front of new people—people without expectations. That's why there are so many stories of juniors who begin a new assignment with a new set of coworkers—and suddenly, they blossom. They haven't magically acquired new skills or chutzpah; they've simply found a new audience.

Organizations can also help professionals get ready for the image-forging aspect of the leap by offering classes, either in-house or out, that develop the more intangible capacities of a senior professional. For example, some firms offer training in self-awareness and professional development. These sessions can make explicit the stages and challenges of forging a new identity.

Training Mentors

Mentoring has always been one of the executive's most challenging responsibilities. Even in the days when the apprenticeship model was firmly in place, many managers struggled with the complicated roles of coaching and teaching, pushing and pulling, holding close and letting go. Today's economic landscape makes it even tougher. In view of the economic opportunities available, partners must be out of the office making rain. The need for mentoring hasn't disappeared—far from it—but the time available to do it has certainly dried up.

Also making it hard for executives to mentor today is the fact that many have simply never been told how to do it. The exact responsibilities and boundaries of the job confuse and sometimes even scare them.

Consider what happened recently when I conducted a workshop on mentoring for an international professional service firm. The workshop was part of the kickoff of a new formal mentoring program. I asked the inaugural group of mentors and protégés to comment on what they hoped to get out of their new relationships and what they feared about the program. The protégés spoke first, enumerating the long list of characteristics their ideal mentor would possess. This person would be wise, successful, wield power in the firm, have extraordinary technical prowess, care about and have time for them, be a nice person, and manage their own life such that work wasn't everything. As the list unfolded, the faces of the assigned mentors showed increasing alarm. When the mentors first spoke, their words were candid: "That is precisely our fear—that you have expectations we could never possibly meet. We don't know how to do this job."

Such confusion hasn't stopped many firms from launching ambitious formal mentoring programs that link virtually every professional in the firm with a more-experienced guide. These initiatives usually fail for one simple reason: chemistry. Chemistry is the key ingredient in true mentoring relationships, but it is most frequently an outcome of working together on real tasks. It can't be mandated by the HR department or a leadership team.

Does that mean throw out the formal programs? No, but firms should reconsider their purpose. The assigned mentor should certainly be a coach, friend, and supporter—the traditional models. But new mentors should also be able to steer the protégé to a broad set of people and experiences until he or she finds a more natural adviser. Programs can also be structured such that the switching costs are low for both protégé and mentor if they choose to find a new match. As a number of prominent professional service firms have discovered, they stand to benefit from providing training to mentors on the basics of their job: helping smart people to learn.

Taking Flight

Nowadays, when people talk about the old economy, it is frequently with a bit of derision. The new economy offers so much more flexibility and opportunity, it is thought. But when the old economy left, it took with it some useful practices, among them, the apprenticeship of young consultants, investment bankers, and accountants during the long journey to partner. That apprenticeship did not guarantee, of course, that every professional made the leap to partner with ease. And in fact some were guaranteed to fail because of tradition and sheer economics. But still, some young professionals were shown the way to the other side of the crevasse.

Today, more than ever, firms need to get their scarce professional talent to the other side, and yet they are hamstrung by partners' lack of time and their knowledge about mentoring itself. Making more time is probably not possible. But it is possible for partners to come to understand the complex and delicate transformation process—the identity forging—that professionals go through as they try to take the leap. And with that understanding, they can help their protégés make the leap and take flight.

Notes

1. These concepts were discussed in Donald E. Gibson's, "Inspiration and Imagination: The Role of Composite Role Models in Organizations," Yale School of Management Working Paper, A91 (1999).

2. See Hazel Markus and Paula Nurius, "Possible Selves," *American Psychologist*, September 1986.

Originally published in March–April 2000
Reprint R00206

Who Wants to Manage a Millionaire?

SUZY WETLAUFER

Executive Summary

NO ONE CAN SAY FOR CERTAIN how many million-aires have been created by Wall Street's long boom. But this new breed of employee certainly creates a whole new set of challenges for managers today. Work-ing millionaires make motivation and retention—two hard games to play in the first place—harder than ever. And they push already steep compensation levels upward. What, then, can be done to manage millionaires in a way to make them worth the effort, not to mention the cost?

To answer this question, Suzy Wetlaufer, senior exec-utive editor of HBR, interviewed more than two dozen CEOs, HR executives, and headhunters from Wall Street and Silicon Valley, as well as a half-dozen working mil-lionaires themselves. Their thoughts—and the managerial imperatives they imply—have culminated in the first HBR at Large, a new department designed to explore multi-faceted business ideas confronting people creating, leading, and transforming business today.

Wetlaufer discovered, somewhat unexpectedly, that many executives see an upside to the rise of the working millionaire. Millionaires force companies to be far more creative—indeed, entrepreneurial—about their products and services. They push companies to keep beating their targets in the marketplace. And they compel their bosses to build a productive, healthy culture.

Admittedly, some millionaires can only be kept happy with corporate jets, original art lining big offices, and world-class executive lunchroom cuisine. Indeed, millionaires are driving managerial practices that, in another time, might have been dismissed but that today are merely admission to the game. But the irony is that such practices should perhaps have been there for everyone all along.

Every now and then, a very talented employee walks into Bob Knowling's office at Covad, the high-flying Internet services company where Knowling is CEO. The employee settles in his chair and smiles. Knowling smiles back. There is little tension, little acrimony. Both know what's coming. The employee wants out. He's bored, needs a new challenge. Or maybe he just needs to rest, see his kids again. In the history of business, these are hardly new excuses for quitting. What is new is how often they're

Millionaires come and millionaires go. The best you can do is to keep them while they still care.

being proffered these days—because they can be. The employees who regularly stop into Knowling's office, like legions of others in the new economy, happen to be millionaires. They don't have to work—and their money changes everything.

Over the next hour or so, Knowling and the departing employee will talk in even, dispassionate tones. Knowling will suggest the employee consider other high-level jobs within the company; perhaps a new leadership role can be created for him. The employee will shake his head no. The company just isn't as exciting as it used to be in its scrappy start-up days, he might say, or an offer to become CEO of a pre-IPO company down the street is simply too good to ignore. Sometimes the departing employee is just weary, and he'll tell Knowling so. He needs time to decompress; he's taking his family on a long vacation, points unknown. Eventually, Knowling will know he's lost the battle, and he'll stand, warmly shake the employee's hand, and sincerely wish him well. Over the past few years, he's learned that millionaires come and millionaires go. The best you can do is to keep them while they still care.

No one can say for certain how many millionaires have been created by Wall Street's long boom, but according to one government survey there were already 4.6 million U.S. families worth more than $1 million by the end of 1998. That number may seem small compared with the general population—it's less than 5% of all families—but the new millionaires tend to be clustered in the industries, namely high-tech and finance, that made them rich. It is well known that roughly 30% of Microsoft's 31,000 employees are millionaires, but that's hardly an exceptional case. At Citigroup, for instance, 150 employees are worth more than $50 million—and about 1,000 people make over $1 million in cash each year, according to two sources close to the investment bank. Even an established company like Wal-Mart, thanks to its practice of aggressively pushing equities down the ranks, has its fair share of millionaires—hundreds alone stocking shelves and unloading pallets.

Civilization depends on "the legal right of the millionaire to his millions," über-capitalist Andrew Carnegie once claimed. And, at least in the current exuberant expansion, few people are disputing that assertion. But millionaire employees, happy though they may be, have a way of making life anything but for their employers. Because they don't have to work, many check out—physically, mentally, or both—long

Millionaires force companies to be far more creative than ever about their products and services—how else to keep the work interesting?

before their work is done. Some take new jobs that seem hotter for some reason or other, an imminent IPO being among the most common. Others simply retire, and still others move on to start their own businesses—to start competing enterprises, in the worst-case scenario.

Those millionaires that don't check out can be remarkably demanding about the nature of the jobs they keep. They ask their bosses to create work that delivers a constant stream of growth and challenge, and sometimes they even ask for work that is, plainly put, mostly fun. Moreover, by some accounts, working millionaires have a tendency to want ever more money. "They always claim the job is never about money, once they're rich," remarks Daniel Meiland, CEO of the executive search firm Egon Zehnder International, which places hundreds of investment bankers and high-tech executives a year. "But as you negotiate the terms of the job, you discover that there is no such thing as enough money any longer. It is a rare person who will take a pay cut for the work alone."

But Meiland, and many other business leaders interviewed for this article, sees an unexpected upside to the rise of the working millionaire. Yes, they make motivation and retention—two hard games to play in the first place—harder than ever. And yes, they push already steep compensation levels upward. But they also force companies to be far more creative than ever, indeed entrepreneurial, about their products and services—how else to keep the work interesting? At the same time, the presence of millionaires on the payroll drives companies to keep beating their targets in the marketplace, for millionaires are highly prone to leave when the team stops winning.

Finally, millionaires simply compel their bosses to be better—more engaged with the work and more inclined to build a productive, healthy culture. The millionaire trend "forces you to be the best manager you can be, or people will just leave," notes Patty Murray, director of HR at Intel. "The bar is higher than ever before. Bosses have to care intensely about strategy, see how everyone plays a critical role in it, and then make that happen. And they really have to understand the skills and talents and needs of their employees, person by person." Murray's contention is echoed by Michael D'Ambrose, head of HR at Citigroup. "What you find today is that what millionaires want is to be treated like individuals. They want to be respected by the people they work for. That means they want their bosses to hear them and make time for them. Does that make Sandy Weill's job harder? You bet it does. Is it worth the effort? Yes, again."

So who wants to manage a millionaire? It is a task so daunting, perhaps no one would want it. But managing millionaires just might have its own rich rewards for the organizations that do it right.

I recently interviewed more than two dozen CEOs and HR executives about the best way to manage millionaires. I also spoke with a number of Silicon Valley and Wall Street headhunters, both to hear what attracts millionaires to companies and what makes them jump ship. Finally, to test what I was hearing about successful approaches to motivation and retention, I interviewed a half-dozen working millionaires themselves. While there was certainly diversity of opinion among all those I interviewed, central themes did emerge.

First, to manage millionaires right, people said, it's imperative to start with a distinct kind of informed hiring. Whether you are hiring people who may become millionaires *because* of your company, or whether you are hiring people who have already made their fortunes elsewhere, go after individuals who want to create a legacy with their lives as much as, or more than, they want wealth. Look for people who want to make a difference—change the world, even. That way, they're more likely to stay, no matter how big the bank balance becomes.

This approach makes sense in theory, but it has a significant problem in practice. It requires employers to look at candidates with the eyes of God—eyes that see into a person's soul. You can certainly try to read a candidate's character, many executives admitted, but it's terribly difficult to do it well, especially in the crush of time. Hiring is hard enough already.

A second theme that emerged in the research was that once millionaires are hired, they need ever changing, ever more difficult challenges—and they need their bosses to get out of their way. You cannot micromanage someone who is, for all intents and purposes, an independent agent. Moreover, millionaires want their challenging, free-agent-y kind of work to take place in a nurturing, even familial, culture. As one Silicon Valley executive put it, they want to take the ball and run with it wherever they please, but they still want to be loved when they lose the race. "Don't we all?" she added dryly. (This executive, like a small number of others I interviewed, asked not to be identified.)

A final theme that emerged had to do with the etiquette of relinquishing millionaires to the marketplace. Executives today, scarred by repeated losses in the talent wars, have learned to say good-bye with as much goodwill as they say hello. It is, they've seen, a revolving-door economy. If companies play it right, their departing millionaires may come back. But for that to happen, they have to leave happy. Indeed, millionaires have to leave so happy, many executives said, that they simply cannot bring themselves to work for a competitor in the interim. That, by the way, is the final insult of the working-millionaire phenomenon—and it happens all the time.

The Blocking and Tackling of Millionaires

Imagine the new economy's talent pool for a moment. Most executives would agree it's small to begin with. There may be a half-million engineers, analysts, and investment bankers swimming around, but, truly, only thousands of them qualify for the Olympics. Now, add the sharks—the countless companies that are desperately hungry for talent. Count to ten and all that's left is pulp.

It is in those waters that executives today go looking for people who "want to build a dream" and "make a difference with their lives." Even if you were to let go of your cynicism and assume that fully half the world longs to leave such a legacy through their careers, current conditions would make those noble folks few indeed. Still, executives seek them out. They study them with X-ray vision, looking for evidence that it's not all about the money. And yet, paradoxically, the lure of millions—or more millions, in some cases—happens to be one of their best drawing cards.

So how do you find them—those rare creatures who don't care about wealth but somehow end up interviewing at companies that offer heaps of it? For Joy Covey, one of Amazon.com's senior-most executives, the key is to listen to the subtext of their conversation.

"Very few people walk into an interview and say, 'I'm only here to make a pile of money,'" Covey says. "But there are subtle signs. Their sensibilities sort of bleed out of them. Very early in the interview process, they are more focused on financial returns for themselves than on the company's vision or mission or their role. They ask a lot about their stock deal. They want to know a lot of details about the structure of their vesting, or they ask, 'Will you buy me out of my current situation?' They're looking for guarantees. You can hear it. And we just can't afford to have those kinds of people join Amazon. They undermine what we're doing, which is building a company for the long term."

Selection is also a defining moment at Covad. "We were growing so fast last year, we hired people with the fog test," admits CEO Knowling, whose company went public in 1999. "You fog the mirror, you're hired." But too many get-rich-quick-then-quit employees forced the company to change its ways, and its turnover rate has dropped from 15% a year to 3%. The solution was to impose a strict discipline around hiring. "We still screen for performance first. But then we screen just as intensely for values. The people we hire have to be passionate about customers; they have to show integrity in everything they do. They have to show a sense of urgency; they have to be performance driven.

"Now, you don't *ask* people if they have these values. Of course, they'll tell you they do. You look for them in the way they've behaved in the past. And, when you're talking with job candidates, you listen carefully for overuse of the word 'I'—'I did this' and 'I did that'—with very little mention of the word 'team.' Believe me, we have found those are very bad signs."

For Tom Tierney, the outgoing CEO of management consulting firm Bain & Company, hiring in an environment where candidates are already millionaires, or intend to be soon, is something of an exercise in identifying each candidate's psychological trip wire. That's the line, once crossed, where people say, "I've got enough." Over the years, after hiring more than 5,000 would-be millionaires, Tierney has learned that some people can live happily with one lonely million in the bank and a fulfilling job. But for others, ten times that still feels paltry, great work or not. For them, money is a way of keeping score. They never have enough if someone else has more. These are the individuals who may sound like the ones to avoid because they are motivated by a thirst no company can quench. Problem is, they sometimes turn out to be the best performers. So he goes ahead and hires them anyway. "You can't really tell up front which is which," he says, "because they don't even know themselves. Always recruit the best—nature will take over from there."

Covey, Knowling, and Tierney agree, however, as did
most executives interviewed for this article, that hiring
for values (if you even can) is, at best, only half the battle—and the easier half at that. Once you've got the millionaires, you must keep them performing at their best.
Like any other employees, they have to hit tough dead-
lines, go to boring meetings, and put up with difficult
clients. Simply put, work needs to get done—and on
Internet time, no less. But unlike other employees, the
millionaires on the payroll can display a certain sense of
entitlement. They'll do the work, but they want their
hearts, minds, and souls engaged, too. It's a classic case
of conflicting needs—the employees versus the shareholders. Or is it?

Management 101

It turns out not to be. Executives may bemoan the trials
and tribulations of managing millionaires, but no one
ever complains that the effort isn't worth it or that it
backfires. In fact, some executives are coming to recognize that the motivation and retention practices they use
for millionaires would keep any employee—rich or
poor—motivated, and hardly at the expense of shareholders' returns. The main difference, and it's not to be
underemphasized, is how much harder and more urgent
these practices become when employees can walk without a second thought. For managers, that leaves almost
no margin for error.

In the final analysis, though, "It actually ends up to be
what might be considered pretty old-fashioned stuff,
what you have to do to manage millionaires," says Dan
Smith, the president and CEO of Sycamore Networks, the
Massachusetts-based maker of optical-networking prod-

ucts, which went public last year in one of the Street's richest IPOs. "Your products have to work. You have to make the right reads on customers. Then you have to execute, execute, execute. Doing very well in the marketplace—being a winner—is the best motivator and retention tool. It's pretty much that simple."

Smith uses Cascade, the high-tech company he ran until July 1998, to make his point. More than 100 millionaires were created by Cascade's IPO. "Lots of people could have chosen to stop working, and to the best of my knowledge, not a single one did. The main reason was that the company had a winning environment. People saw their work as directly contributing to the success of Cascade. People see the work they are doing is defeating the competition and keeping customers satisfied." That phenomenon, of course, puts enormous pressure on senior management to keep overall performance sky-high. Smith is unfazed by that fact. "You don't really have a choice," he notes. "If you are not performing well, a cloud hangs over the organization. People say, 'Why bother working here?' and they start to leave."

Smith names one other key management practice he uses to motivate millionaires—the shortest possible feedback loop. "It's an epidemic in large companies—people don't see the whole that they are working on. They can't tell if their work on any given day was good or bad. I mean, in a typical large company, people can be assigned to a product development program and not know for a year if it has succeeded or failed. That's demoralizing." By contrast, Sycamore is made up of five "minicompanies," each focused on a distinct optical-networking platform and market segment, whose activities are reviewed weekly or, for some projects, even daily if need be. Feedback from customers, through sales and support activities, is also immediately brought back into the organization. In this way, the engineers within each minicompany can see within days whether their efforts are working or not.

"To keep our elite performers, people who could literally work anywhere, or not at all, we have to keep re-creating for them the conditions that brought them to a start-up in the first place."

"People should always know what they're working on and why, and they should always be in a position to understand how their work makes a difference and feel its immediacy," says Smith. "That's true whether they're millionaires or not, but it's more important when people *need* reasons to come to work every morning."

If Smith designs the work at Sycamore to feel immediate and meaningful, other executives design it to feel constantly fresh and challenging. "We know we can't forever retain all of the top talent that joins Priceline," says John Patterson, the vice president for talent at Connecticut-based Priceline.com, which has about 400 employees. "The best we can do is to predict with a certain degree of accuracy who is mission-critical to the business and what it would take to keep them. And to do that, our leaders have to be eyeball to eyeball with them, making sure their work is exciting. When it's not anymore, I know they're at risk."

Indeed, Patterson says, Priceline has a business model geared toward competing in the war for talent. When a new business opportunity is identified, it's added or spun off, providing top talent with new opportunities within the Priceline family. "To keep our elite performers—people who could literally work anywhere, or not at all—we have to keep re-creating for them the conditions that brought them to a start-up in the first place. We create smart new projects for people. We let them run whole new enterprises or launch something international. We have to let them stay in control of their careers, because once they feel like the company is driving them, instead of the other way around, they leave."

"When you're talking about keeping people who could leave at any moment, pick your battles."

Such an approach, Patterson notes, is not for everyone. It would be too expensive. With the salaries people command today, companies have to get laser focused on identifying top talent and then meeting their professional and psychological needs—and theirs alone. "I cringe when I hear HR people say, 'Let's give retention bonuses to everyone.' That's wrong," Patterson says. "Better to take the money and energy and focus it on the people who make the business happen. For everyone else, make sure they are learning, contributing, and having fun. Make sure they know what opportunities are available throughout the company. But when you're talking about keeping people who could leave at any moment, pick your battles. You can't fight too many at once—you need to focus on retaining *critical* talent."

Like Priceline, Intel also aggressively uses varied assignments to motivate and retain its employees. "Moving people around is part of our fabric," says Murray, the HR head. "We start with the assumption that people work to be challenged, and so that's what we do, over and over again."

Case in point is Louis Burns, who joined Intel 18 years ago as a technical field salesman. For four years, Burns worked as an individual contributor in St. Louis, then moved to head up the regional technical sales operation out of Dallas. A few years later, Burns was leading the worldwide technical sales business from California.

Then one day, Burns's boss unexpectedly approached him about moving over to IT. "That was a whole new set of problems and players," recalls Burns. "I had no idea if my skills and experience would apply. That was scary, but I was determined to try." Four years later, Burns was running all of Intel's IT operations. Then, opportunity knocked again. Burns was asked to run Intel's Platform Components Group (PCG), the company's primary producer of core logic and integrated graphics chip sets. "I didn't even think about it. I just said yes," Burns recalls. "My heart was beating fast, and the prospect of leading a product group felt like a big unknown. That's what told me it was the right thing to do." Burns has now been running the PCG business for a year, knowing full well he'll eventually move on to another part of the company.

Somewhere along the way in his Intel career, Burns realized that the financial benefits of working at Intel were secondary to him. "It has never really been about the money for me. It's nice to have, but once you have it, the work is what matters. It forces you to get clear and to ask yourself, 'Why do I do this every day?' And when you can answer that with, 'Because I love it,' you can feel very good about getting out of bed in the morning."

Challenging work, however, appears not to be enough to motivate millionaires. They also need to be left alone to do it. People who have independence in their personal lives are almost never inclined to surrender that autonomy at work. That's a lesson Bob Knowling almost learned the hard way when he tried to micromanage a talented, and extremely wealthy, senior executive at Covad. "I was all over him," recalls Knowling, "and he was ready to quit. That was my wake-up call. Even though I am a hands-on guy, I now keep my distance from my people. You have to give people space and room to perform their duties. I stay attached without being intrusive by checking in for updates and through dialogue—a few times a week for some, less frequently for others. I have had to let go of my ego and let people do their own jobs. In this environment, a CEO can only be a coach, enabler, and a mentor. Otherwise, you give people ammunition to leave, and they don't need much."

Just That—and More

Is that all then? Just a winning environment, immediacy, meaning, challenge, and freedom? Is that *all* there is to motivating and retaining the wealthiest of employees? The final answer is...no.

No, because after all the other demands comes culture, already the bugaboo of executives everywhere. Millionaires want, it ends up, just what every other employee wants—an organization that loves, nurtures, and forgives them. An organization that delights and celebrates them. They want a corporate good mother. The only difference between them and their less-affluent siblings is that they can run away from home if she doesn't come when they cry.

Most executives want to create a positive culture, millionaires or not. They know its virtues. But until now, they've often been able to let culture slide as a top priority. No longer. Today, companies meet the needs of their millionaires with countless ways of making them feel deeply connected, bonded in a warm web of mentoring, parties, and group trips.

But that's not all. Many companies trying to create a culture conducive to keeping millionaires have found themselves offering the kinds of day-to-day lifestyle benefits that only the very rich could come to expect. At Citigroup, for instance, executives eat in a dining room tended by world-class chefs. They can easily book the corporate jet to make *"Hierarchy never made* their long business trips *anyone feel good, except the* less exhausting, and they *people at the very top."* are encouraged to make their offices as luxurious and personalized as their own homes. "If people want artwork, we make it available. If they want a couch, we're ready to meet their individual needs," says D'Ambrose, the HR head. "We want to make this a great place to work. The environment has to make people not consider the value proposition of working somewhere else or of not working at all."

Bain, too, is famous for the energy it devotes to creating a culture no one wants to leave. "Voice mail and e-mail aren't enough to create connection," says Tierney. "People have to know each other. They have to work and play together." To that end, Bain sponsors a near-endless stream of social and business events—white-water rafting trips, off-site training sessions, picnics that feature the homegrown Bain Band, now in its twentieth year of performing at company functions. Once a year, the company holds its own version of the Academy Awards, where staff members select the best client success story from 50 nominees. "We want to keep creating a real celebratory, high-fiving kind of culture," says Tierney, "because that feels good for the people who work here, and it translates into results for our clients. But cultures don't just happen. They take work."

Cole Peterson, executive vice president of the People Division at Wal-Mart, agrees. "We work on our culture constantly. Take the language we use. Language is powerful and it telegraphs a lot about your beliefs. We prefer the word "coach" rather than "boss." Everyone is an associate; hierarchy never made anyone feel good, except the people at the very top. To reinforce this, we have what we call our 'Open Door Policy': If you have a concern about your work environment, store, or area, you can talk to anyone, at any level, in this company about it. Your concerns will be kept confidential, if you choose. That allows a very strong flow of information upward. There's no question that listening can take a great deal of time, but it gives you all that you need to fix things and make good decisions. You'll get a very strong and healthy culture, and culture is your best path to retention."

Such Sweet Sorrow

But in the end, sometimes even a healthy culture can't retain everyone, Peterson acknowledges. "Some people will want to start a dot-com themselves or simply look for a change. Giving them more money or a different job within the organization is not the answer," he notes. "At a certain point, you shouldn't try for retention anymore. They're meant to leave."

Thus comes the challenge of managing millionaires out the door.

"Just last month, one of our brightest, brightest guys said he was leaving. We had already redesigned his job for him twice, but the company had outgrown him. He needed a start-up again," says Knowling. "Now, I was distraught, but I'm of the Jack Welch school of thought on this one. You don't say goodbye. You say, 'Until we meet again.' I asked for his résumé. I told him he could come back in a heartbeat, and then I told his new CEO he had a terrific person working for him."

The point, says Knowling, is to leave people feeling great about your company so they won't join a competitor or start one themselves.

A less radical alternative to saying farewell is to invite people who are trying to quit to go part time, quit slowly, or take a sabbatical. Consider what happened five years ago when one of Chase H&Q's best investment bankers told CEO Dan Case he was retiring. "I told him he wasn't allowed to leave. We needed him. His clients needed him. And I had this sense that, maybe, he still needed us a little, too," recalls Case. "I said, 'Become an advisory director. Come and go as you please.'" He really rejected the idea at first. He said, 'Forget it. An advisory director is an old person no one listens to.'"

But Case's flexible exit strategy finally won over the banker. Over the years, he did deals he chose to work on, which ended up to be more than he expected. In fact, in 1999, the man, already a millionaire many times over, posted his best year ever, and he remains a valued mentor to Case and others. "Let's just say he's retiring at his own pace," Case says.

Bain, too, offers a flexible quitting plan. Employees on the verge of exiting are allowed—even encouraged—to work for other companies and come back when they feel ready. Paid sabbaticals are available to partners who have typically worked at the firm for five to six years. And just recently, the company began a new venture,

The Bain Bridge Group, a consultancy for nonprofit organizations, where current and former employees who want a new professional focus or are financially secure—or both—can spend a year or two, for a change of pace and perspective. "At some level, this all is very altruistic," says Tierney, "but on another level, not at all. It's smart business. You've got to give people opportunities to pursue their passions. If they leave, our job is to treat them as valued alumni—and perhaps they will return."

The Rich Leading the Rich

Throughout my interviews, one aspect of the working millionaire phenomenon went unspoken: millionaires today are almost always being managed by people who are millionaires themselves. That's the nature of compensation through stock options. And so, while many executives in my research talked about how difficult it is to motivate and retain individuals who are extremely demanding and often very fickle, they invariably did so without resentment, without even a hint of frustration. These managers and their millionaires are, after all, kindred spirits. In some sense, they are even equals. It just might be that all those millionaires out there are, at last, ushering in what has been ballyhooed for a long time in business—the true end of hierarchy.

It seems likely, then, that the complicated pas de deux between millionaires and their managers will continue as long as the economy permits. There will be no overthrow of the system by the "laborers," no crackdown by the bosses. Instead, companies will continue to keep their millionaires happy with managerial practices that, in another time, might have been dismissed as outrageous or servile. Today, they are merely admission to the game. And the irony is, perhaps they should have been for everyone, all along.

Originally published in July–August 2000
Reprint R00412

Too Old to Learn?

DIANE L. COUTU

Executive Summary

C.J. ALBERT, THE HEAD OF family-owned Armor Coat Insurance, is just settling in on a Sunday evening when he receives an unsettling phone call from his star salesman. Fifty-two-year-old Ed McGlynn has just returned from a business dinner with his younger technology mentor, and he's none too happy with the way he's being treated. If C.J. doesn't take this attack dog off him, Ed warns, he's gone.

C.J. had indeed assigned 28-year-old Roger Sterling—the company's monomaniacal, slightly antisocial director of e-commerce—to teach Ed about digital strategy and the Web. Reverse mentoring seemed like a good way to create synergy between the sales and technology groups. The goal was to create a digital insurance product that would allow Armor Coat to keep up with its competitors.

But there'd been tension between Ed and Roger right from the start—stemming from their personalities and their two departments. So when the two reluctantly agreed to meet for dinner to talk, the conversation didn't go well. Ed insisted that great sales reps, not the Internet, are crucial to selling insurance. Roger insisted that the Web will revolutionize the way insurance is sold and distributed—that Ed either give in or move on. Ed took off in a huff and subsequently phoned C.J. Roger followed Ed's irate call with his own weary ultimatum: "Either Ed goes or I go."

C.J. faces some difficult Monday-morning discussions with both disgruntled parties. What should he do? Six commentators, including a mentor-protégé pair, offer their advice in this fictional case study.

C.J. LOVED *LAW AND ORDER*. He seldom had time to watch TV anymore, but when he did, he wanted something unsentimental. As a rerun of the show came on, he settled into the taupe leather sofa in the living room and adjusted his glasses. Just then, the phone rang.

Even now that he was CEO of Armor Coat Insurance, the Providence, Rhode Island-based property and casualty insurance company that he had inherited from his father, there was still one thing that C.J. could not do— let a phone go unanswered. Not even on a Sunday night. He sighed and picked up the receiver.

"C.J.? I've been looking everywhere for you." The voice at the other end of the line was angry and intense, and C.J. knew instantly that it belonged to Ed McGlynn, the company's star salesman.

Ed had been named top performer six of the last ten years and had pulled in most of Armor Coat's major accounts. Customers loved him. At 52, he was still the magnetic and popular hockey hero that he had been at Notre Dame. He took his major clients sailing on weekends and played golf with them during the week. Whenever he recounted his triumphs, Ed would brag about how more than 300 of Armor Coat's customers had sent him get-well cards after he'd had his appendix out. Now, on the phone, Ed was clearly upset.

"I've been with this company 23 years, and I've given it everything I've got," he fumed. "But if you don't get rid of that SOB you sicced on me, I'm out of here. Those Internet guys don't speak the same language we do. They're arrogant. They lack respect. They don't have the same values. And I'll tell you, C.J., I'm not just some stupid salesman who's going to sit back while some baby-faced know-it-all squeezes the life out of me."

New Tricks of the Trade

The know-it-all was Roger Sterling, the 28-year-old Web guru that C.J. had hired last year to be the director of electronic commerce at Armor Coat—and the mentor that C.J. had assigned to work with Ed on his computer skills.

With his entrepreneurial flair, and a monomaniacal focus on business, Roger seemed typical of the breed of software engineers that flourished in Silicon Valley. He had studied math at Cal Tech for a year and was second in his class before he dropped out to join a $20 million start-up. Born with a sense of entitlement and a conviction that the rest of the world was irrelevant, Roger had a reputation for his technological savvy—and for his nonexistent people skills. After the IPO, he was not only richer but also brasher than before.

Roger took the job at Armor Coat only because he was convinced that the insurance industry was ripe for an e-commerce revolution. Insurance was, after all, a product that consisted purely of information and money. Already, he understood the possibilities of the Internet the way few people in the insurance industry did. For him, it was simply a game to push the technology to its limits—without regard for the people who would use it. When C.J. approached him about restructuring a national program to sell insurance directly to customers on the Web, Roger knew exactly what the potential was: "We can eliminate about 2,000 agents. It's a license to print money."

The odd thing was, Roger had a hard time understanding why some people might object to a cavalier attitude like his. C.J. chalked it up to generational differences. If Roger had emotions, he hid them well—so well that the senior salespeople called him "Pac Man." His robotic reputation was only reinforced by the fact that he didn't seem to have any outside interests. He didn't play sports, he didn't fish—he didn't seem to do anything but drive to and from work in his BMW convertible.

"Yes, if I could invite only one of the men to my club, it would definitely be Ed," C.J. said to himself. And now Ed's ego clearly needed massaging. C.J. sympathized with his star salesman—he himself knew little about computers. But at the same time, he realized there was no going back to the predigital age. Armor Coat had to move into the Web era or it would die.

Legacy of Change

Indeed, change had been the norm at the French-Canadian company that the Albert family had founded as a four-man operation in 1879. Since then, Armor Coat was where all the Albert men had cut their teeth. A few old hands still remembered C.J.'s legendary grandfather Anatole, who had run the company with an iron fist. But it was C.J.'s father who had done the most to make the company what it was today: a nationally recognized corporation with offices in 32 states. By the time C.J. took the helm in the late 1980s, Armor Coat's sales and profits were skyrocketing. The company finally went public in 1996.

The IPO had made the Albert family extremely rich—C.J. himself was a millionaire many times over. Still in the afterglow, C.J. knew that the family and other shareholders trusted him to keep things on track. That meant staying devoted to the customer and keeping costs down. The latter was especially challenging given that many traditional insurance firms were considering going on-line. Internet-only start-ups had already discovered cheaper, more efficient ways to replace the ingrained and expensive agent networks, and C.J. knew that Armor Coat could ignore this option only at its peril.

Armor Coat needed to draw on Ed's strength in customer relations and on Roger's strength in cutting-edge technology.

Yet no company to date had found a way to overcome the customer's desire for human contact. It was understandable that people might not want to buy insurance—a product often associated with death and disaster—through an impersonal intermediary such as a computer. The challenge, as C.J. saw it, was to find a way to make the digital product friendly and unintimidating. To do that, he reckoned, Armor Coat needed to draw on both Ed's strengths (solid customer relationships) and Roger's (cutting-edge technology). The older generation and the new needed to come together to make this work.

That wasn't going to be easy. There'd been tension between the company's salespeople and Roger's department right from the start. Internet experts didn't come cheap. In fact, C.J. had to offer them salaries that were equal to the money being paid to sales agents who had already been in the field for 15 or 20 years. It was inevitable that those agents would resent the "overpaid" newcomers. C.J. also decided that the new Web designers would report directly to Roger. C.J. realized that Roger's management position could stir angry feelings among the salespeople and concerns about company priorities. But he knew the new technology recruits would need lots of support and responsibility if the transformation was really going to work. All that was bad enough, but then C.J. fired 10% of the sales force to cut costs. The reaction was severe: the survivors felt betrayed. The salespeople blamed the Web designers for the organizational grenade that had been tossed into their midst.

Who's in Charge?

C.J. had hung up the phone and was sitting on the sofa, deep in thought. His wife Karen walked into the living room, noticed that the TV was on mute, and read her husband's expression. "What's wrong?" she asked. Karen was a child psychologist and the mother of their two children, Annie and Simon. C.J. and Karen had been married almost 25 years, and she knew everything there was to know about him and the business.

"Things are coming unglued," C.J. sighed. "Ed just called, and he's hopping mad about some blowup he had with Roger Sterling. I'm beginning to give up hope that this mentoring thing is ever going to work between them."

C.J. picked up the remote control again and returned to the last moments of *Law and Order.* Just before the end, a commercial came on for on-line stock brokerage Ameritrade. It featured a young office worker whose boss interrupts him from photocopying his face for party invitations—not to reprimand him but to ask for his help buying stocks on-line. The young guy shows his boss how to navigate the Web—and then explodes into an exuberant dance and invites his boss to the party.

"Like it or not, it's the younger generation that will have to mentor us rather than the other way around," C.J. mused. "And that's a big problem for guys like Ed."

"Well, it certainly isn't working out that way at Armor Coat, is it," C.J. blurted, lifting himself off the sofa and walking across the room to the bookshelf. He picked up a volume of the *Encyclopaedia Britannica* and absent-mindedly flipped though the pages. "Like it or not, it's the younger generation that will have to mentor us rather than the other way around," C.J. mused. "And that's a big problem for guys like Ed. He's so proud—and so suspicious of technology. And so reluctant to change. But change is the only thing kids know."

A New Kind of Mentor

C.J. had, in fact, tried to do exactly what the Ameritrade commercial had depicted. Armor Coat's HR department earlier in the year had initiated a reverse-mentoring program: all salespeople were strongly encouraged to choose a young mentor who could teach them how to store and call up information from Armor Coat's new on-line databases and how to surf the Web. The thought was, if the customer-focused salespeople understood the Web more, they could help Armor Coat use the Internet to boost profits and improve service.

When C.J. discovered that Ed had failed to pick a mentor, he decided to assign Roger to work with him. What Roger lacked in people skills, he made up for in sheer smarts and in his interest in insurance—two virtues that Ed admired a lot. C.J. even dared to hope that Ed would be flattered to get one-on-one attention from the company's tech guru.

"Give Ed space to ask you naive questions. He's got to learn about things he's not familiar with," C.J. counseled Roger. "But listen to his questions, too, because he knows a lot about our customers."

Roger was less than optimistic. He thought the whole experiment was a waste of time. "What's at stake is not a few computing skills but the fact that guys like Ed have to learn to think about the business in an entirely new way," he told C.J. "Ed needs a complete change in mind-set, and I can't manage that by teaching him a few tricks on the computer. In themselves, computer training classes are pointless."

The relationship didn't get better from there. Only last Monday, a furious Roger had called C.J. to complain that Ed had skipped a critical meeting outlining how the Web would create a more efficient interface between insurers and their customers. "That fast-talking jock isn't a team player," Roger protested vehemently.

C.J. didn't have time to deal with the call just then. The board meeting was coming up, and he was deep into preparing a presentation on the company's quarterly results—which for the first time in 12 years were dipping. "Can't you guys work out your differences?" he asked. "Just sit down and try to work through the problem." When Ed rang three minutes later to complain about the same meeting, C.J. blew up."I don't want to hear about it anymore. My God, Ed, you're twice his age. Fix it!"

The Dinner That Didn't

Reluctantly, Roger and Ed agreed to meet at the Wild Ginger that Sunday night to try to patch things up. It was the first time they had ever sat down for a meal together, and Ed was late. He'd been shuttling his kids back and forth to soccer games all day, and he was tired.

When he got to the restaurant, Roger was already seated at a table, sipping green tea. "Ah, you're drinking my daughter's favorite," Ed said, trying to make small talk. "She's quite the computer one, she is." Roger smiled politely but said nothing. Ed found his irritation mounting at the company for putting someone as socially inept as Roger Sterling in a position of authority.

He ordered a double shot of Jameson's, and then unfolded his chopsticks and started delicately poking around at the eel and California maki that Roger had ordered as an appetizer. Ed was the first to broach the subject. "C.J. said we should get together and try to iron out some of our differences," he said, weighing every word. "Maybe for the sake of Armor Coat, we can make some of these innovations work."

Roger's response was quick and nonchalant. "They *are* working," he said. "I told C.J. that. We're right on course. My team is getting things done even faster than scheduled."

Roger's retort made Ed clench his fists under the table. "I'm not stupid, Roger," his voice shook. "I may be many things, but I'm not stupid. The Web is changing distribution, yes, but great sales reps are and always will be the key to the insurance business. People don't buy insurance—you sell it to them. They don't think about their mortality—you gently remind them of it. I know how this business works. I've been doing it since before you were out of diapers."

Roger had heard this story before, and his eyes moved up when waiters passed by the table. Ed was deeply annoyed by Roger's reaction but pressed on. "Let's put our cards on the table," he said finally. "I don't like the way you and the other 'whiz kids' have been treating us in sales. You're condescending. You routinely schedule meetings on short notice without even checking whether it's a good time for us. You don't respect our experience."

Roger leaned in toward Ed. "Look," he said, trying to be conciliatory, "I'm not saying work in the field doesn't pay off. But I don't think you realize how much the customer's mentality is changing. People want information fast. They want to be able to compare the numbers and the services, and that's a lot easier to do on-line. As I see it, you have two options: you can join the team, or you can leave the team. It sounds brutal, but the younger people in sales are *getting* it."

Ed was horrified. "Let me give you some advice, kid," he said, reaching for his wallet. "Don't ever go into PR." Ed slammed enough cash on the table to cover dinner for both of them. He pulled his coat close to his chest, turned on his heel, and stormed out of the restaurant.

"You're a million miles away," said Karen, turning off the TV while C.J. was still flipping through the encyclopedia.

"I was just thinking that mentoring seemed so much easier in my day when it was clear who did what," her husband explained. "Wisdom got passed down through the generations. But these days it's people who've dropped out of school who have the edge."

"I don't think it's all that strange," Karen countered. "We learn from our kids, don't we? And I always learn from my patients."

"Yeah, but when we were kids, Karen, I was an expert on stamps. You were an expert on Nancy Drew. Today's kids are experts on a global revolution that is affecting every aspect of our lives. No wonder Ed feels like he's losing control." Just then, the phone rang again. This time it was Roger. He sounded tired—and fed up. "C.J., I'm a digital expert, not an expert on fixing the egos of insecure, middle-aged salesmen. That's just not what I came to Armor Coat for. Either McGlynn leaves the team, or I do. That's *your* decision. I'll be around tomorrow if you want to talk."

C.J. replaced the phone in its cradle and relayed the latest news to Karen. "What am I going to do?" he asked with deep frustration in his voice. "I don't need a generation gap at Armor Coat. I need these guys to connect. Otherwise, we won't be here in five years."

What Should CJ Do?

Six commentators offer their advice

MONICA C. HIGGINS *is an assistant professor of organizational behavior at Harvard Business School in Boston.*

The events at Armor Coat do not describe mentoring, reverse or otherwise. We have a situation in which a young new-hire has been charged with teaching a salesman who has been with the company 23 years how to surf the Web. If it works, such a program might constitute coaching of some sort, but it is certainly not true mentoring, which involves both career and psychosocial support, such as friendship and caring.

At bottom, this case is about organizational change—about a successful, family-run insurance business that needs to change the way it delivers services to customers. To effectively move Armor Coat in a new direction, C.J. Albert should be leading the charge. Instead, the CEO delegates the organizational change effort to Roger Sterling—a newcomer who does not seem to care about anything except money and technology. This is both unrealistic and bound to fail.

It's no surprise that at the end of the case, we have two valuable employees, Roger and Ed McGlynn, who are both ready to leave the company in a huff. The attempt to institute a reverse-mentoring program has clearly failed. Let's see why. From the case, we know that C.J. has appointed Roger to mentor Ed. Yet research suggests that a mentoring relationship works best when it evolves over time, in an informal fashion, through a shared interest in professional development. This was clearly not the case at Armor Coat.

Other research shows that effective mentoring relationships are those in which the communication styles of the mentor and protégé match one another. Here, the opposite is true. Ed enjoys interacting one-on-one with people, developing such strong relationships with his clients that they send him get-well cards. Roger has a robotic style. Clearly, this was not the right match—much less the right conditions under which C.J. could have ever expected a true mentoring relationship to flourish.

Beyond his poor understanding of mentoring relationships, C.J. seems oblivious to the emotional fallout from the change effort at Armor Coat. His own diagnosis? "Generational differences," he says, and at one point he even orders Ed to "Fix it!" This diagnosis does not address the real problem: as Ed clearly tells Roger at their ill-fated dinner meeting, the senior sales staff feels that its experience is not respected.

Ed's feelings are certainly not the bailiwick of *any* generation, be they 20-somethings or 40-somethings. Yet his complaint underscores a fundamental problem in this case: no change program can succeed simply by imposing a mechanistic mentoring program from above on employees who are struggling with a widespread transformation effort and who lack genuine respect for one another.

Perhaps it is C.J.'s wife Karen who understands best what's at stake. She recognizes that Armor Coat will have to integrate the young people if it is going to change. But she doesn't see anything fundamentally new about that. She always learns from her younger patients, she says. So, too, in today's information-based economy, knowledge may be king, but it's the sharing that takes place between young and old that is essential.

C.J. will need both Roger and Ed to change Armor Coat. But before any sort of meaningful change effort— or even mentoring—can get under way, C.J. needs to exercise real leadership. He already understands that both Roger and Ed have their strengths, but he has failed to communicate that. He can begin there—it's not too late. After all, both men have turned to him for advice and counsel. Now it's C.J.'s turn to mentor.

LLOYD TROTTER *is the CEO and president of GE Industrial Systems in Plainville, Connecticut.*

There's an obvious lack of fit between Roger Sterling and Ed McGlynn in the reverse-mentoring program at Armor Coat, and C.J. should take immediate steps to end that relationship. But the trouble at Armor Coat goes deeper than a personality clash between these two men.

Roger is not just a poor mentor, he is also an employee who is out of sync with the company's core values. His attitude does not mesh with the values of teamwork and camaraderie that have long driven corporate culture at Armor Coat. So apart from the mentoring question, C.J. has to decide whether or not to keep Roger.

Just as important, C.J. has to find some way to undo the damage to Ed. His top salesperson's ego and self-esteem have been badly bruised. Given the current business pressures, C.J. can't afford to have Ed become disengaged. Alienating him could have devastating effects on his productivity and, ultimately, on the company's bottom line. Ed's situation must be addressed as soon as possible.

But Ed should get more than fuzzy words of reassurance from C.J. He deserves assistance in his efforts to accommodate all the changes that are currently unfolding at Armor Coat. At GE, we've learned that if an executive closes himself off from learning new things, he is putting his career in jeopardy—and the company's success at risk. Ideally, there should be an intervention from human resources.

After resolving these issues, C.J. has to reposition reverse mentoring more positively to his employees. To a large extent, it seems as though the program was created from the top down and forced on warring camps in the company. The business has a rich family history and a strong work ethic, so it seems as though Armor Coat's employees would more likely accept reverse mentoring if it were positioned as a tool for collaboration rather than as an us-versus-them blockade.

Armor Coat also needs to reexamine how it matches individuals. The company must take into account the dynamics of the people involved in the reverse mentoring relationship. C.J. needs to seek out best practices from other companies. How do they screen mentoring candidates? What personality traits make the best matches? What should the expectations be on both sides of the relationship?

Lastly, the idea of reverse mentoring needs to be introduced prudently. I know that when I was presented with the possibility of having a younger person mentor me, I found it a bit daunting at first. But for both of us, the reverse-mentoring program at GE has been an excellent tool for mutual learning and growth. I believe that the key to our success is that no matter at what level we find ourselves in the organization, we can accept change. Those who cannot become obsolete in our organization.

Meeting with my mentor has made us both more ready for change, and we quickly recognized numerous learning and teaching opportunities that cut both ways.

I've learned a lot about the Internet from my mentor, and I've been able to experience and see firsthand the bright, young talent that represents the future leadership of my business. At the same time, my mentor has had a tremendous opportunity to learn what it's like to be a CEO. If we had both closed ourselves off from these experiences, it would have been a senseless waste. That's how I see it for anyone who is not open to learning—top down or bottom up. It's slamming down the gate on your own future.

It's not too late for C.J. to make reverse mentoring work at Armor Coat. By learning from this experience, he can begin to develop some best practices that will not only help his company become an e-business but also raise the bar for other companies that want to launch a reverse-mentoring program.

STEVEN LURIA ABLON *is an associate clinical professor of psychiatry at Harvard Medical School and at Massachusetts General Hospital, both in Boston. He is also a training and supervising adult and child analyst at the Boston Psychoanalytic Society and Institute.*

My father, who was the CEO of a *Fortune* 500 company, often told me that progress occurs when old men die and young men take over. I argued the point with him. My view is that real progress occurs when people are open to learning from mentors, regardless of their age. And an essential characteristic of good mentoring is openness, by both parties, to the complexities of the other person's experience.

At Armor Coat, neither Ed nor Roger has any real interest in trying to understand the other's experience. We don't know exactly why, but it may have to do with their own vulnerable self-esteem or how they identify with authority figures, such as parents or siblings.

Whatever the reasons for the antagonism between Ed and Roger, it's up to C.J. to find a creative way to help his employees work together. By sending the two men out to dinner alone, C.J. abdicated his responsibility. Rather than assume that he understands their experience, he should sit down with them and immerse himself in their viewpoints.

C.J. needs to establish an environment in which Ed and Roger feel comfortable sharing their experiences and concerns. By fostering such an exchange, C.J. would be mentoring his two subordinates by letting them see the importance of openness and co-mentoring. He could then use that experience to demonstrate to Ed and Roger how the two men can learn from each other—and turn Armor Coat into a company that makes the best use of the old and new economies.

Let me use a clinical experience to illustrate how this can work.

In my work as a child psychoanalyst, I always learn from my patients. One such patient was a ten-year-old named Harry. His parents brought him to me because over the course of a year, Harry had looked sad, was often tearful, and was constantly daydreaming in class. After Harry got to know me and began to feel comfortable in the office, he told me he wanted to play chess. He announced that he was very good at chess. We played the game several times, and it turned out that his way of playing the game was quite unusual. Whenever he faced a difficult situation, he would announce a new rule that gave his pieces unusual powers. Then he would defeat me soundly.

As the games continued, Harry told me that the queen was actually a very weak piece. He explained that the queen was weak because she had to spend so much time watching out for the king, who really could do very little for himself. Over time, Harry and I came to understand how the game related to his life. In the past year, his father had developed asthma and on several occasions had life-threatening attacks. Harry's mother lived in terror that her husband would die suddenly. She gave up her usual activities in order to be available in case of an emergency. In this context, family life became chaotic and confusing. Harry felt that his home life had become unpredictable and precarious.

Harry and I were mentors to each other. I learned from Harry that he didn't need help with the rules of chess or to be able to accept losing; he needed someone to understand the broader experience at the root of his behavior. At the same time, Harry began to realize that I was interested in exploring and understanding his conflicting and confusing feelings and experiences. He learned that I wanted to understand him, not judge him.

If they are to learn from each other, Ed and Roger need to try to be open in a similar way. They need to understand that by working together and embracing their differences they will ultimately be able to harness each other's strengths to help build a successful business. They both have unique contributions to offer. But to have any chance of working well together, they're going to need C.J. to step in and lead by example.

Learning about the complexity of another person's experience is essential in all relationships and crucial for a vital and satisfying life. Although I don't always agree with my dad, I've learned a lot from him over the years. Understanding our differences brings us even closer.

STUART PEARSON *is marketing services IT manager for Procter & Gamble in the United Kingdom and Ireland.*

MOHAN MOHAN *is vice president of the health and beauty care division of P&G in the United Kingdom and Ireland.*

The real problem in the reverse-mentoring relationship between Ed and Roger is the huge amount of fear and insecurity in both players. C.J. may not be able to salvage them as a team, but he may be able to use the conflict to learn valuable lessons about the nature of mentoring and change.

The brash, steely-eyed but technologically brilliant Roger actually has a lot to teach Ed about competing successfully and profitably in the networked economy—despite what Roger thinks about computer training being "pointless." It isn't just by luck that Roger has positioned himself as a Web guru in an industry that is ripe for an on-line revolution. He is not afraid of change or hierarchy, and in our experience that's a good trait for young mentors to have. Reverse mentors can't be easily intimidated; they need the self-confidence to set challenges for their protégés or the relationship won't work.

Roger's role as mentor should be to stoke Ed's enthusiasm for technology—but C.J. also needs to convince Roger that he, in turn, has something to learn from Ed. Without this mutual deference, no mentoring relationship can ever work, reverse or otherwise.

This is where Roger's lack of people skills gets him in trouble. Not only is he unable to increase Ed's comfort level with technology, but Roger seems uncertain whether he even wants to reach out to Ed. At this point, C.J. must convince Roger to step back from his mission of pushing technology to its limits and take stock of the interpersonal factors at play. That would be a big first step toward improving the relationship.

Of course, Ed has his own issues that he has to come to terms with: there are the new-hire salaries, the layoffs in the sales department, and perhaps even fears about growing older. And although Ed is great at what he does—the numbers show that—he is unwilling to learn how to conduct business in a changing electronic world. All his antics, from bailing out of a training session with Roger to failing to pick a mentor in the first place, point to a man who is afraid to change his good-old-boy ways of selling insurance.

Ed may never become a technology expert, but he needs to take a more proactive approach to getting this new training and information. This is where HR could help, perhaps by creating a customized program to introduce Ed to the technological skills he so badly needs.

No matter what happens to Roger and Ed, C.J. shouldn't give up on the concept of reverse mentoring—it can be a powerful tool. But C.J. should realize that mentoring has a delicate bond at its core—one that can't be forced. P&G's reverse-mentoring program is voluntary, and it has worked beautifully time and again. Even though the working relationship between the two of us fit into an overall training initiative here at P&G, we originally came together because we wanted to, not because we were assigned to one another. We arrange mutually convenient times to meet. We don't consider the age gap a burden but an opportunity that enriches our business and personal relationships— whether we are talking about PalmPilots or work-life balance.

The reverse-mentoring program at P&G has another benefit—it spreads the knowledge base throughout the company, which is crucial to any organization's success. There are many ways to get conversations going in a company, but reverse mentoring is one of the best. And all it takes is a genuine willingness to learn.

Indeed, our own experiences with reverse mentoring at P&G have been deeply guided by Alvin Taylor's observation that "in the twenty-first century, an illiterate is not one who cannot read or write, but one who is unwilling to learn, unlearn, and relearn."

YORAM "JERRY" WIND *is the Lauder Professor of Marketing at University of Pennsylvania's Wharton School in Philadelphia. He has been leading the development of the Wharton e-Fellows program, which includes a reverse-mentoring component that matches senior executives with Wharton students.*

C.J. must be extremely frustrated after getting off to such a promising start with his efforts to bring Armor Coat into the digital era by creating an "unintimidating" on-line insurance product. He hired a highly qualified technology person, Roger, and empowered him to lead the company through its Internet revolution. He rightly recognized the need to integrate Roger's on-line expertise with Ed's understanding of customers' needs—and instituted a reverse-mentoring program to create that synergy.

But despite his best intentions, C.J. now has a couple of extremely unhappy players on his hands—high performers who represent the two functional groups that lie at the core of C.J. and Armor Coat's e-transformation strategy.

So what happened? As I see it, there are three fatal flaws in C.J.'s strategy. First off, the CEO planned to implement companywide change through the functional silo of technology rather than through a cross-functional team.

Next, he neglected the organizational architecture. He failed to alter the culture and the compensation systems so they could assist the e-transformation at Armor Coat.

Finally, C.J. didn't create an effective reverse-mentoring program.

Reverse mentoring, to work effectively, should be a nonthreatening, supportive, and educational experience for both parties. So the selection of a mentor is as critical as the choice of a coach in any professional sport; it requires careful thought and consideration. For instance, you wouldn't have Andre Agassi coach Pete Sampras while the two still compete aggressively against each other. Assigning Roger to coach Ed is just as inappropriate.

From Ed's perspective, Roger is the enemy. His arrival prompted the layoffs of Ed's friends and colleagues, and his impersonal way of transacting business goes against everything that Ed believes in. From Roger's perspective, Ed is not a colleague in need but someone who stands in the way of progress.

Given the intense opposition of these men, the relationship forced by C.J. was bound to fail.

The mentor and protégé must share a common objective, and there must be trust between the two parties. The right mentor for Ed would be a young person with expertise in technology—and someone who can show empathy and interest in Ed's mastering the technology necessary to take Armor Coat into the next millennium. The mentor should also show a healthy respect for the skills that Ed brings to the table. Given his personality, maybe Roger should not mentor at all.

A final point: reverse mentoring can solidify collaboration among functional groups, but it cannot be the only tool that enforces such teamwork or the sole catalyst for change, as seems to be the expectation here. Rather, effective reverse mentoring is a by-product of good communication that already exists between functional groups. Even the best mentor-protégé relationships have their limits.

Originally published in November–December 2000
Reprint R00605

Managing Away Bad Habits

JAMES WALDROOP AND

TIMOTHY BUTLER

Executive Summary

WE'VE ALL WORKED WITH HIGHLY competent people who are held back by a seemingly fatal personality flaw. One person takes on too much work; another sees the downside in every proposed change; and a third pushes people out of the way. At best, people with these "bad habits" create their own glass ceilings, which limit their success and their contributions to the company. At worst, they destroy their own careers.

Although the psychological flaws of such individuals run deep, their managers are not helpless. In this article, James Waldroop and Timothy Butler—both psychologists—examine the root causes of these flaws and suggest concrete tactics they have used to help people recognize and correct the following six behavior patterns:

The *hero*, who always pushes himself—and subordinates—too hard to do too much for too long. The *meritocrat,* who believes that the best ideas can and will be determined objectively and ignores the politics inherent in most situations. The *bulldozer,* who runs roughshod over others in a quest for power. The *pessimist,* who always worries about what could go wrong. The *rebel,* who automatically fights against authority and convention. And the *home run hitter,* who tries to do too much too soon—he swings for the fences before he's learned to hit singles.

Helping people break through their self-created glass ceilings is the ultimate win-win scenario: both the individual and the organization are rewarded. Using the tactics introduced in this article, managers can help their brilliantly flawed performers become spectacular achievers.

We've all worked with people who are star performers but have one serious personality shortcoming that makes life difficult for everyone, limits their effectiveness, and often proves to be their professional undoing. One person, for instance, constantly takes on too much work. Another scorns the behind-the-scenes politicking needed to win support for most projects. A third sees the downside in every proposed change. In the words of one executive we worked with, such people are "95% brilliant, 5% disaster."

We call these destructive behavior patterns "bad habits" as a shorthand way of referring to deep-rooted psychological flaws. In other words, we're not using the term to describe compulsions like smoking or nail biting. Nor are we applying it to people who—at one time or another—bully coworkers, struggle with self-doubt, or drive themselves too hard. No one is perfect; we all wrestle with demons and make mistakes. Instead, we're using the term to talk about employees whose psychological makeup translates into consistently problematic behavior. Their "bad habits" are a central part of their personalities and inform the way they behave from day to day. At best, such people create their own glass ceilings, limiting their success and their contributions to the company. At worst, these otherwise highly competent and valuable people destroy their own careers.

Although the psychological flaws of such individuals run deep, their managers are not helpless. There are tested, effective ways to help people recognize and correct their bad habits. Over the course of almost 20 years of research and practice as business psychologists and executive coaches, we have identified 12 discrete patterns of behavior, or habits, that lead to these career troubles. Managers have a greater degree of leverage helping people whose behavior fits the following six patterns:

The Hero always pushes himself—and, by extension, subordinates—too hard to do too much for too long.

The Meritocrat believes that the best ideas can and will be determined objectively and thus will always prevail because of their clear merit; ignores the politics inherent in most situations.

The Bulldozer runs roughshod over others in a quest for power.

The Pessimist focuses on the downside of every change; always worries about what could go wrong rather than considering how things could improve.

The Rebel automatically fights against authority and convention.

The Home Run Hitter tries to do too much too soon—in other words, swings for the fences before he's learned to hit singles.

Let's be clear: we're not urging managers to get advanced degrees in psychology or to put their employees on the couch. But like it or not, managing today involves more than shuffling the right bodies on the assembly line; it requires knowledge of minds and hearts. Your only choice is between being a good "psychologist" or a bad one.

Being a good psychologist doesn't mean you have to explore your employees' complicated past to figure out exactly why they act the way they do. In fact, if an employee tells you "it all began when I was abused as a child," it's time to call in a professional. But you can use proven tactics to help the hero, the bulldozer, the pessimist, and the others become much more effective employees.

Our emphasis is on the practical. We have written in the past about retaining top talent (see Chapter 8, "Job Sculpting: The Art of Retaining Your Best People"). This article focuses on helping your star performers be most effective.

Helping people break through their self-created glass ceilings is one of the ultimate win-win scenarios you will encounter as a manager. When a member of your team reaches his or her potential, both the person and the organization are rewarded. We understand that this work requires precious time and energy on your part, but we're confident that the benefit to your organization will provide a better return than many other investments you could have made with your time. (Sometimes, however, it's better not to make the investment. Not everyone will respond, and it takes an ongoing effort. To perform a preliminary ROI analysis, see "Is It Worth the Effort?" at the end of this article.)

Root Causes

We have deliberately described the bad habits in our typology in simple, concrete terms. But it's useful to know a bit about the fundamental psychological processes underlying these behaviors. They grow out of a mix of an individual's genes and environmental influences, such as family and peer relationships. In one combination or another, these processes come together and lead some people into destructive behavior patterns. As a manager, you need only keep the processes in the back of your mind. Your goal isn't to offer counseling but to help your employees control the specific behaviors threatening to destroy their careers. You'll find that this objective is quite ambitious enough.

The four psychological processes underlying the bad habits are:

An inability to understand the world from the perspective of other people. An astonishing number of people have difficulty getting outside their own frame of reference and seeing through another person's. In other words, they lack empathy. In a sense, they never moved beyond the narcissism that is normal in childhood; they never got the instruction from parents or others that helps most people learn to understand the world from other people's perspectives. Having a well-developed sense of empathy is essential if one is to deal successfully with one's peers, subordinates, managers, customers, and competitors.

A failure to recognize when and how to use power. Many people feel a deep ambivalence about the utility and value of power. These feelings often stem from unconscious fears of our capacity for destructiveness. The fact is, many people confuse using power with abusing it. As a result, they either avoid gaining power altogether or they acquire it but then fail to use it—and power is a "use it or lose it" phenomenon. Of course, there are some people who are all too happy to obtain power, which they then wield like a cudgel instead of a surgeon's knife. In short, a great many businesspeople haven't done the hard work of figuring out how to use power effectively.

A failure to come to terms with authority. Most of us are ambivalent about authority. As children, for example, we often rebel against our parents even as we want to remain under their protection. Some people get stuck at one of the extremes. At one end are those who defy authority in every possible instance and in every possible way. At the other end are those who are overly deferential: "If top management says it's true, it must be." Most people fall somewhere in between. For example, in our experience, people like the idea of having a mentor but rebel when they actually have one.

A negative self-image. Poor self-esteem can come from various factors. Some people feel pressure from our achievement-driven culture to accomplish more—and to do it faster—than their peers. The possibility of failure is always looming. Other people's self-esteem deficiencies stem from mild to moderate levels of depression. Whatever the deep-seated reasons, building a career on a foundation of poor self-esteem is equivalent to erecting a skyscraper on sandy soil.

And yet, this psychological flaw undermines the confidence of a surprising number of businesspeople, from first-time managers to CEOs. One CEO of a successful high-tech firm who had unconsciously set himself up to be fired later admitted that he just never felt like he belonged "with the real grown-ups." It's not that he—or anyone—should always feel invincible. The goal is to be able to act effectively while accepting your inevitable shortcomings and life's disappointments.

That goal, in fact, is what drives our advice on how to help flawed performers overcome their bad habits. We'll look closely at each behavior pattern in turn.

The Hero

The hero is often the last person a manager wants to change. After all, why would you want to tamper with the behavior of someone who gets more done in a day than anyone else does in a week? The answer is that over the long term, the hero's constant pushing adds real costs to the bottom line—even if those costs are obscured by short-term results. If you look carefully at the hero's trail, you'll probably find the footprints of valuable people who left the company after trying to keep up with the hero's superhuman exertions. Within the company, you'll find burned-out coworkers. And the hero himself may be thoroughly spent, too.

People who habitually push themselves and others to the breaking point do so for various reasons. Some heroes become addicted to success at a very early age; others push and push as a way of dealing with their own shaky self-esteem. An "I'm gonna show them" mentality vis-à-vis authority is common. Clearly, heroes lack the empathy needed to understand what others are going through to keep up the pace.

To change a hero's behavior, start by expressing your appreciation for his accomplishments. But don't linger on that point—quickly segue into a discussion about the costs of burnout. Talk with the hero about recognizing the signs of overload in himself and in his team members. Make it clear that this is a very serious problem—that the hero has consistently taken things to a point at which more is not better. He needs to put on the brakes.

The hero must learn how important it is to take regular readings of his team's temperature. There are obvious physical cues: bags under the eyes, stifled yawns. In meetings, heroes need to learn to pay attention to body language, facial expressions, and energy levels that subtly indicate resistance or dismay.

As the hero's manager, you may want to help him make a checklist of warning signs that the temperature is getting too hot. The list might include the times that he and others are leaving voice messages and e-mails, the number of cars in the parking lot after 9 PM, rising levels of illness among employees (especially the number of people who come in even when they're sick), and reports of marital troubles. The hero should fill out the list weekly and discuss it with you.

Heroes have to think more about winning the war and less about the individual battles. A good general knows when to pull back to fight another day. Accordingly, you should reward the hero for actions that demonstrate a long-term focus and reprimand him for going to short-term extremes. We know of one case, for example, in which a hero was taken to task for making his team come in over the Fourth of July weekend. Emphasize that you need your hero to make strategic decisions; he should delegate the implementation whenever possible.

You might encourage him to hire an assistant with both the confidence and the mandate to rein him in when he is driving too hard.

If your hero regularly intrudes on subordinates' time at home, you may need to ban him from contacting them at night or on weekends. If that seems unduly strict, you could require him to make explicit that he doesn't expect a response until the next day or after the weekend.

Finally, it is essential that someone take on the official role of observing the hero. The goal in dealing with this bad habit is to turn down the volume without switching it off. That's why you need someone with normal hearing to help the hero adjust the level. You could decide to do this yourself at least part of the time. Even so, it's a good idea to solicit another view. You can help your hero choose a trusted coworker to carry out this task. At least initially, that person should help the hero take his team's temperature. Most people are reluctant to tell the hero directly that they're tired and need a break.

Changing heroes' behavior is a delicate proposition. After all, you want heroes to continue to do all the good things they've been doing. At the same time, you have to let them know that there's nothing heroic about driving themselves and others into the ground. Careful "fine tuning" of these important contributors is essential.

The Meritocrat

Meritocrats earnestly believe that the world is a fair market in which the best ideas will always win on their own merit. Such people typically excelled at school. They were the outstanding test takers who were consistently rewarded for getting the highest score; thus they have a naive reliance on the authority of objective, measurable facts. They never accepted that in the real world, ideas have to be sold, negotiated, and shaped to meet political and organizational realities. You have to be willing to horse-trade and to accept solutions that don't give you everything you want. People who don't accept these basic facts won't be as effective as they could be—in any situation.

Hal, for example, was an equities analyst at a New York investment bank. He was a quantitative whiz—he could tear apart a balance sheet faster and better than anyone else on the floor. But he would seethe when people challenged his analysis of a company or ignored his recommendations, especially when they acted only on their gut feel for the market. Likewise, when less bright but more politically savvy peers were promoted ahead of him, Hal was infuriated. These reactions, of course, were part of the reason he wasn't promoted. Hal's meritocratic behavior sabotaged his career.

To help a meritocrat, you should first offer sympathy. Go ahead and agree that it's really an awful waste of time to have to persuade people to support ideas of clear merit, to have to trade your quid for their quo, to tiptoe around certain sleeping dogs while throwing meat to others—and most of all, that it's too bad that we even have to spend our time having this discussion. In an ideal world, personal feelings and loyalties would have no place in decision making.

The next step is to raise a very difficult, but very important, question: how effective do you want to be? We've done this ourselves by using Jimmy Carter as an example. Carter, we say, was a highly principled and intelligent president who stayed unswervingly true to his ideals. And yet even the most die-hard Democrat would agree that Ronald Reagan was more effective than Carter at winning congressional and public support for his agenda. We ask, "Do you want to be 100% pure, like Carter, or do you want to be effective, like Reagan? You must choose one or the other."

Why even bother having this conversation? Because meritocrats are typically among your hardest-working, brightest, and most well-educated people. A manager needs to help them see that it is possible to operate in gray areas, accomplish a great deal, and still emerge relatively unsullied—say, 90% pure.

Give the meritocrat a little time to absorb this message, but don't let him drown in self-pity. Instead, jump to something concrete: "So, let's turn to that great initiative you mentioned to me last week. Let's do it. Who do we need to get on board to accomplish your goal? Whose opposition do we need to neutralize? What trade-offs do we have to make? How can we sell the idea to the final decision maker? Is there anything we should ask for now with the intention of giving up later?" And so on.

The point is to communicate that the business of actually getting things done is exciting and challenging—it's playing a game where the results really matter. Nothing is quite as satisfying as feeling personally effective, and that is what the meritocrat—with all his line-in-the-sand bravado—is likely to have missed out on. Once he has a taste of success, he'll usually want another—and the second time around it will all come more naturally to him.

Like the hero, the meritocrat has to learn much more about his team. For each member, he needs to ask himself, What does this person work for—big money, prestige, intellectual challenge, acquisition of power? What does this person most like to do—solve problems, think about the big picture, call the shots? And how does this person work—with attention to detail, by intuition, by networking, or alone in a quiet space? Only when the meritocract understands and takes into account individual differences can he figure out how to get people to support his goals and make their strongest contribution to a project.

Understanding and accepting the personal factors that influence decision making is difficult at first. As the meritocrat's manager, you need to help him begin to see them objectively, as no different from any other factors being considered. Not everyone will come around to that view, of course. Some will prefer to move on to other places in search of a true

Bulldozers are often reluctant to change a style that, by their lights, is highly effective. So to change a bulldozer, you have to become one yourself.

meritocracy. Ultimately, however, the thrill of victory will be enough to persuade all but the most intractable meritocrats to change their behavior.

The Bulldozer

Bulldozers are people who decided early on that the world is a hostile place where you should do unto others before they do unto you—plus 10%. They intimidate and alienate everyone in their path. They don't trust others, and others don't trust them. At the same time, they're extremely loyal to their bosses, and they get things done—which is why they're worth trying to help.

Bulldozers are often reluctant to change a style that, by their lights, is highly effective. So to change a bulldozer, you have to become one yourself. Start by asking him if he has any idea how many enemies he has created within the company. Follow this with a powerful line we've used in our consulting: "If I put it to a vote, there's no question—you'd be fired."

A bulldozer will protest that you're being unfair. The right response is: "Look, I don't care if you think you're the gentlest person on earth. It doesn't even matter if I agree, because other people don't. And it's like being a stand-up comedian—if you think you're funny but the audience doesn't, you're not."

It helps to have some concrete evidence: "Did you notice in the meeting yesterday that after you finished questioning Joanne, no one said a word?" or "Here are some ways people describe you: cruel, mean-spirited, somebody I would never turn my back on." (We've heard all these comments made about bulldozers.) To get past a bulldozer's denial, it's often necessary to deliver the ultimate message: "I'm not going to baby you. You're costing me too much. Change or find another job."

The threat of being fired is usually quite motivating. If the bulldozer now indicates that he's willing to listen, the next step is to begin a campaign of rapprochement. Tell the bulldozer to make a list of his victims—people he has angered in the company. If he stumbles—if the list is too short—help him complete it. The bulldozer should then rank them from most damaged to least. Choosing the least-offended person first—in other words, the easiest to confront—the two of you should then script out (literally, on paper) an apology that *must* contain the words "I'm sorry."

Trivial as this may sound, it is essential that apologies be made for past misdeeds; and it will not be easy. To get your bulldozer used to saying the magic words, offer to role-play the part of the person he is going to try to make peace with. The odds are that the list of people deserving apologies is a long one, so he will get plenty of practice, but the first step is always the hardest. Offering apologies en masse won't smooth over all the damage, but it's a necessary first step.

The ultimate goal, of course, is to get the bulldozer to avoid causing damage in the first place. To do that, he has to become more aware of when he is about to roll over someone—what muscles tense up, what thoughts start to run through his head—so he can stop himself. He may have to take a break during a meeting or, in a conversation with an individual, pretend to have just remembered a call he has to make. These simple tactics actually work.

Your initial confrontation of a bulldozer needs to be strong and direct. It's also important to confront a bulldozer as soon as possible after seeing him in action; he'll start to recognize internal cues if you can point out external actions when they are still fresh in his mind. (This goes for all the bad habits. Like the clues in a crime scene, people's memories fade quickly. Time is your enemy when you're trying to help someone reconstruct what happened.) As with a hero, it's a good idea at the beginning to agree on someone the bulldozer trusts to monitor his behavior. If the bulldozer shows a willingness to change, he'll be able to build roads for you without flattening people in his way.

The Pessimist

Pessimists have nothing but the best intentions. Their goal is to preserve the organization from the harm that could come to it because of ill-advised change. The problem is, pessimists think *every* change is ill advised.

Pessimists' worries are sometimes justified—they're based on a knowledge of mistakes that others have made in the past. More frequently, though, pessimists simply stifle creativity and block fruitful opportunities. They also tend to micromanage, looking over everyone's shoulders lest a mistake be made.

Pessimists are motivated primarily by a fear of shame—of being wrong or inadequate. And avoidance of shame can spread insidiously throughout an organization's culture, becoming an unconscious modus operandi that has disastrous results for the company's capacity to innovate and take risks.

Pessimists not only ignore the potential upside of change, they also usually fail to consider the downside of doing nothing.

Fortunately, there are tactics that managers can use to change the pessimist's nay-saying. Begin by telling the pessimist that you're on his side in looking at proposals for change with appropriate caution. That positioning lets you avoid a pointless wrangle over the pros and cons of any particular initiative. Then point out that, as in the children's story of the boy who cried wolf, you're afraid that the impact of his alarms is diminishing. Moreover, he's giving the other members of his group a free ride: "They don't have to worry, and they certainly don't have to express their reservations. They've delegated that to you." The message is, it's okay to worry, but it's important that your fears do more than guard the status quo; they should have a constructive edge.

One way to make the pessimist's worry into a more effective tool is to teach him how to evaluate risk better. Pessimists not only ignore the potential upside of change, they also usually fail to consider the downside of doing nothing. Tell your pessimist that in the future, when a change initiative is proposed, he should draw a two-by-two matrix that looks at the pros and cons of making the change as well as the pros and cons of doing nothing. By making this systematic consideration of initiatives into a routine, the pessimist will be forced into a more objective risk analysis.

As a final step, you could offer to protect the pessimist from every kind of risk except one. Consider this example. One of our clients, an executive at a commercial bank, used almost those exact words to help a subordinate who said no at every opportunity. Our client finally said to him, "Look, we've got to take some risk when we lend money—that's why we get interest!" He helped the subordinate think about risk in a new way by telling him this: "If you try something new and fail, I'll take the blame. If you try something new and succeed, you'll get the credit. But if I find that you're refusing to take risks or getting in the way of others who have good ideas, you'll be held accountable." The pessimist got the message and learned to look at risk with more clarity.

In chess, fighting every game to a draw is not the objective; the goal is to checkmate your opponent. The pessimist must understand that you are playing to win, not to stay even. There are no draws in today's economy.

The Rebel

Teenagers imagine that they are rebelling by wearing funky clothes and getting outrageous haircuts. In reality, most are simply conforming to the look of their peers. Workplace rebels can also be quite conventional in their knee-jerk reactions against the status quo. Although they fancy themselves as revolutionaries, most of their protests against "the system" don't go beyond simple grousing—they rarely take action to change the things that bother them.

Rebels are easy to recognize. They're the ones who always ask the inappropriate questions in meetings, constantly make jokes about the company's management, and publicly question the motives behind any major change. Their cubes are papered with Dilbert cartoons, and their adherence to company rules is always just to the letter, never to the spirit. In short, rebels do enough to threaten morale that an effort to correct their behavior, assuming that they are otherwise valuable to the company, is a necessity.

What rebels enjoy most is a game of tug of war. So your first tactic is to refuse to play. Don't lose your temper; don't respond to provocation. You can then use two approaches to help the rebel break out of his negative behavior pattern.

The first is to co-opt the rebel by making him responsible for a relatively high-profile task that requires him to win the cooperation of others. In essence, you pull him out of the heckling audience and push him on stage, into the spotlight. The chance to take on an interesting and important project is, essentially, a bribe. Some rebels will see it as such but will take it anyway. Others will stubbornly refuse—in which case, on to the second approach.

Begin by asking the rebel, in a neutral tone and without warning, if he's thinking about quitting. When he— in a state of shock now—says no, tell him that you were wondering because he always seems to be butting up against the limits, venting his frustration, and putting the organization down. If he responds with "No, that's just my way of talking; I'm only kidding around," come back forcefully: "I don't buy that. And in any event, the things you say hurt people and the morale of the group. That needs to stop."

Then shift to a different gear: "But more to the point, you seem to think that a lot of things around here should be changed. True?" The rebel is likely to give some kind of affirmative response. At that point, throw down a challenge: "Well, right now you're about as effective a revolutionary as my three-year-old. All I have to do is tell him *not* to do what I actually want him to do, and he does it. And vice versa. Now, if you're going to battle the counterproductive aspects of the 'regime,' do you want to do it effectively, like a real guerrilla? Or do you just want to be the one who makes an impassioned speech before he gets dragged off to the firing squad?"

The latter is an unappealing option, so now you have the chance to help your rebel become a real leader of change. His first assignment should be to spend a week or two as a cultural anthropologist, noting all the subtle elements of your organization's culture: the way people dress and speak to one another; how much they reveal about their personal lives; how they align in groups; how decisions are made officially and how they are really made; who has informal power and influence, and so on. You should require him to hand you a written report at the end of this period.

Once the rebel has gathered that information, ask him this: "If you were a real revolutionary fighting somewhere against a dictatorship, would it be better to stand out or to blend in?" The answer is clear, so push the rebel to the logical conclusion. "You have a choice. You can work to change things here or you can follow your old pattern and just be an irritant. If you choose the latter, your career will stall and your influence on the organization will never amount to much. I hope you make the other choice, because you're right—this place isn't perfect, and we need people like you to help improve it."

The story of Charlotte, a young manager who was hired at a large insurance company, illustrates our point. She was appalled by the condescending attitude that senior management displayed toward the rank and file. Her response was to tweak the nose of the institution by dressing much more casually than other managers and taking her lunches with the frontline workers. When her manager discussed her behavior with her, Charlotte

Home run hitters tend to strike out a lot, swinging for the fence when a simple base hit would have helped the team just as much.

determined that she wanted to work to change the company's culture. And she did. Instead of "acting out" by dressing down, she directly confronted peers about their superior attitudes. (Ultimately, however, she found the pace of change too slow and moved on to work in another industry.)

A rebel who genuinely cares about the company (and his career) will see the light. Instead of being negative just for its own sake, he'll turn his energies toward constructive criticism and the building of a better company. He won't change overnight, and for some time you'll have to keep a close eye on the situation through frequent meetings. The payoff will make it worthwhile, however.

The Home Run Hitter

The home run hitter is the person who is always imagining the roar of the crowd when the ball clears the outfield fence. In business terms, he imagines his picture on the cover of *Fortune* as the founder of the hottest dot-com, or he sees himself making partner in record time by landing the biggest client. The problem is—going back to baseball—the home run hitter tends to strike out a lot, swinging for the fence when a simple base hit (or even a walk) would have helped the team just as much. Put simply, home run hitters focus on things that are too big too soon.

As a home run hitter's manager, you need to deliver two messages. Number one, you appreciate his drive, ambition, and self-confidence. Number two, you want to move him up the curve as quickly as possible but at a pace that ensures his steady progress.

Your home run hitter should understand that you're not holding him back because his abilities are suspect. In fact, you already see him as very successful—and right on track. Of course he wants to be at the top now; that's only natural for a high achiever. But you have confidence that he will get there if he stays with the program.

The next step is to explain just what the program is. It might include spending time overseas, working more with particular clients, and getting involved with the company's Web initiatives. It's useful to look at people in positions that he aspires to and explain their career trajectories; that way, he'll understand that they didn't just walk in off the street and take over.

Home run hitters worry that they'll never get ahead, and they feel that their strenuous efforts to reach the top go unappreciated. Therefore, it's important to talk with them often about their career progression and to praise them frequently—for small accomplishments as well as for large ones. Those actions on your part will help reassure your home run hitter that, given a little time, he'll have his shot at the big leagues.

John, for example, is a software engineer whose ambition and impatience were leading to bad choices. He was preparing to leave his current company—unwisely, we thought. We encouraged him to voice his concerns to his manager and to initiate more frequent "How am I doing?" meetings. Through those meetings, John gained a broader perspective, letting him see his manager's investment in his success. John just hadn't been able to visualize his career track. Armed with a new appreciation for the value of his work, he decided to stay with the company.

In an economy driven by the knowledge in people's heads, all good managers have to think like psychologists in order to maximize the potential of their people. You don't have to fix people's deep psychological problems, nor should you be trying. As a manager, your ultimate concern is with their actions and results. Although the tactics we recommend here won't work in every case (some people don't really want to change; others have damaged themselves too much within your organization to be salvageable), the approaches we describe are effective with many people. They can help turn your brilliantly flawed performers into spectacular achievers—to the benefit of themselves and your company.

Is It Worth the Effort?

BEFORE TRYING TO HELP ONE of your flawed stars correct his bad habits, you need to make a crucial decision: is the person valuable enough to warrant the investment? In other words, Should you try to help him or should you "manage him out"?

To answer that question, consider the possible outcomes. The best-case and worst-case scenarios are fairly obvious. The most likely result, however, is that the person will take your cue and make an effort to change but will never altogether eradicate the problematic behavior. What is your threshold for a "good enough" recovery? At what point does the cost-benefit ratio move in your favor? Bear in mind that if you expect perfection, you are setting everyone up for failure.

You also need to ask yourself if you are the right person to try to help the employee change. Even if you recognize one of the behavior patterns in someone who reports to you, you may not feel comfortable dealing with it. Maybe you don't have the time or the energy; perhaps the person works off-site. In either case, you can get help from your HR department or from a highly experienced business psychologist or executive coach, both entirely acceptable responses.

If you want to go ahead on your own, plan the initial meeting carefully. Make sure you schedule enough time to discuss the situation thoroughly. You don't want to open up this topic unless you have the time to explore it fully.

It's important that you express clearly the reasons you believe your star performer falls into a particular behavior pattern. Make some notes beforehand so you can be specific and direct. Fresh, concrete evidence is best. For example, "In our meeting with Don, you interrupted him several times when he was explaining his concerns about your plan" or "I've asked you on three occasions now to sit down with Theresa and discuss her workload, but you haven't; you just keep piling it on her." You should also suggest some specific ideas to help the person change the behavior; these ideas will be fleshed out and modified during the conversation, but it's important to have a starting point. Finally, make time for a follow-up meeting soon after the initial discussion, preferably about a week later. Your work to help someone change a behavior pattern isn't a onetime operation. Bad habits take years to develop, and they won't change overnight.

Originally Published in September–October 2000
Reprint R00512

Job Sculpting

The Art of Retaining Your Best People

TIMOTHY BUTLER AND

JAMES WALDROOP

Executive Summary

HIRING GOOD PEOPLE IS TOUGH, but keeping them can be even tougher. The professionals streaming out of today's MBA programs are so well educated and achievement oriented that they could do well in virtually any job. But will they stay? According to noted career experts Timothy Butler and James Waldroop, only if their jobs fit their *deeply embedded life interests*—that is, their long-held, emotionally driven passions. Butler and Waldoop identify the eight different life interests of people drawn to business careers and introduce the concept of *job sculpting*, the art of matching people to jobs that resonate with the activities that make them truly happy.

Managers don't need special training to job sculpt, but they do need to listen more carefully when employees describe what they like and dislike about their jobs. Once managers and employees have discussed deeply embedded life interests—ideally, during employee performance reviews—they can work together to customize future work assignments. In some cases, that may mean simply adding another assignment to existing responsibilities. In other cases, it may require moving that employee to a new position altogether.

Skills can be stretched in many directions, but if they are not going in the right direction—one that is congruent with deeply embedded life interests—employees are at risk of becoming dissatisfied and uncommitted. And in an economy where a company's most important asset is the knowledge, energy, and loyalty of its people, that's a large risk to take.

By all accounts, Mark was a star at the large West Coast bank where he had worked for three years. He had an MBA from a leading business school, and he had distinguished himself as an impressive "quant jock" and a skilled lending officer. The bank paid Mark well, and senior managers had every intention of promoting him. Little did they know he was seriously considering leaving the organization altogether.

H IRING GOOD PEOPLE IS TOUGH, but as every senior executive knows, keeping them can be even tougher. Indeed, most executives can tell a story or two about a talented professional who joined their company to great fanfare, added enormous value for a couple of years, and then departed unexpectedly. Usually such exits are written off. "She got an offer she couldn't refuse," you hear, or, "No one stays with one company for very long these days."

Our research over the past 12 years strongly suggests that quite another dynamic is frequently at work. Many talented professionals leave their organizations because senior managers don't understand the psychology of work satisfaction; they assume that people who excel at their work are necessarily happy in their jobs. Sounds logical enough. But the fact is, strong skills don't always reflect or lead to job satisfaction. Many professionals, particularly the leagues of 20- and 30-somethings streaming out of today's MBA programs, are so well educated and achievement oriented that they could succeed in virtually any job. But will they stay?

The answer is, only if the job matches their *deeply embedded life interests*. These interests are not hobbies— opera, skiing, and so forth—nor are they topical enthusiasms, such as Chinese history, the stock market, or oceanography. Instead, deeply embedded life interests are long-held, emotionally driven passions, intricately entwined with personality and thus born of an indeterminate mix of nature and nurture. Deeply embedded life interests do not determine what people are good at— they drive what *kinds* of activities make them happy. At work, that happiness often translates into commitment. It keeps people engaged, and it keeps them from quitting.

In our research, we found only eight deeply embedded life interests for people drawn to business careers. (For a description of each one, see "The Big Eight" at the end of this article.) Life interests start showing themselves in childhood and remain relatively stable throughout our lives, even though they may manifest themselves in different ways at different times. For

Job sculpting is challenging; it requires managers to play both detective and psychologist.

instance, a child with a nascent deeply embedded life interest in *creative production*—a love for inventing or starting things, or both—may be drawn to writing stories and plays. As a teenager, the life interest might express itself in a hobby of devising mechanical gadgets or an extracurricular pursuit of starting a high school sports or literary magazine. As an adult, the creative-production life interest might bubble up as a drive to be an entrepreneur or a design engineer. It might even show itself as a love for stories again—pushing the person toward a career in, say, producing movies.

Think of a deeply embedded life interest as a geothermal pool of superheated water. It will rise to the surface in one place as a hot spring and in another as a geyser. But beneath the surface—at the core of the individual—the pool is constantly bubbling. Deeply embedded life interests always seem to find expression, even if a person has to change jobs—or careers—for that to happen.

Job sculpting is the art of matching people to jobs that allow their deeply embedded life interests to be expressed. It is the art of forging a customized career path in order to increase the chance of retaining talented people. Make no mistake—job sculpting is challenging; it requires managers to play both detective and psychologist. The reason: many people have only a dim awareness of their own deeply embedded life interests. They may have spent their lives fulfilling other people's expectations of them, or they may have followed the most common career advice: "Do what you're good at." For example, we know of a woman who, on the basis of her skill at chemistry in college, was urged to become a doctor. She complied and achieved great success as a neurologist, but at age 42 she finally quit to open a nursery school. She loved children, demonstrating a deeply embedded life interest in *counseling and mentoring*. And more important, as it turned out, she was also driven by a life interest in *enterprise control*, the desire to be in charge of an organization's overall operations. It was a long time before she stopped remarking, "All those years wasted."

Other people don't know their own deeply embedded life interests because they have taken the path of least resistance: "Well, my dad was a lawyer." Or they've simply been unaware of many career choices at critical points in their lives. Most college seniors and new MBAs set sail on their careers knowing very little about all the possible islands in the sea. And finally, some people end up in the wrong jobs because they have chosen, for reasons good and bad, to follow the siren songs of financial reward or prestige. Regardless of the reason, the fact is that a good number of people, at least up until midlife, don't actually know what kind of work will make them happy. (For more on the importance of life interests, abilities, and values in job satisfaction, see "It's a Matter of Degree" at the end of this article.)

Let's return to Mark, the lending officer at a West Coast bank. Mark was raised in San Francisco; his mother and father were doctors who fully expected their son to become a successful professional. In high school, Mark received straight A's. He went on to attend Princeton, where he majored in economics. Soon after graduation, he began working at a prestigious management consulting firm, where he showed great skill at his assignments: building financial spreadsheets and interpreting pro formas. As expected, Mark left the consulting firm to attend a respected business school and then afterward joined the bank. It was located near his family, and because of its size and growth rate, he thought it would offer him good opportunities for advancement.

Mark, not surprisingly, excelled at every task the bank gave him. He was smart and knew no other way to approach work than to give it his all. But over time, Mark grew more and more unhappy. He was a person who loved running his mind over and through theoretical and strategic what-ifs. (After college, Mark had seriously considered a career in academia but had been dissuaded by his parents.) Indeed, one of Mark's deeply embedded life interests was *theory development and conceptual thinking*. He could certainly excel at the nitty-gritty number crunching and the customer service that his lending job entailed, but those activities did nothing for his heart and soul, not to mention for his commitment to the organization.

Fortunately for both Mark and the bank, he was able to identify what kind of work truly excited him before he quit. Consulting a career counselor, Mark came to see what kind of work interested him and how that differed from his current job responsibilities. Using this insight, he was able to identify a role in the bank's new market development area that would bring his daily tasks in line with his deeply embedded interests. Mark's work now consists of competitive analysis and strategy formulation. He is thriving, and the bank is reaping the benefit of his redoubled energy—and his loyalty.

Career Development: Standard Operating Procedure

As we've said, managers botch career development—and retention—because they mistakenly assume people are satisfied with jobs they excel at. But there are other reasons why career development goes wrong. The first is the way jobs usually get filled, and the second is the fact that career development so often gets handed off to the human resources department.

Most people get moved or promoted in their organizations according to a preset schedule—a new assignment every 18 months, say—or when another position in the company opens up. In either case, managers must scramble. If six employees are all scheduled to get new assignments on August 1, for example, a manager has to play mix and match, and usually does so based on abilities. Who is likely, the manager will ask herself, to do best in which jobs? Similarly, when a position opens up and needs to be filled right away, a manager must ask, "What skills does the job require? Who has them or seems most likely to develop them quickly?"

Sometimes people move up in an organization because they demand it. A talented employee might, for example, inform his manager that he wants to graduate to a new role because he's not growing anymore. The typical manager then considers the employee's skills and tries to find a place in the organization where they can be applied again, this time with a bit of "stretch."

One manager went through three companies before realizing it wasn't the company he needed to change but his work.

Stretch assignments, however, often do little to address deeply embedded life interests. A research assistant at an investment management firm who performs well can stretch her skills into a credit analyst role, and after continued success there, she can move into the position of fixed-income portfolio manager. But what if her deeper interests are in managing others? Or how about the "spot news" reporter who is "stretched" into management when her real passion (discovered, perhaps, through a few years of misadventure as a manager) lies in investigative reporting?

Skills can be stretched in many directions, but if they are not going in a direction that is congruent with deeply embedded life interests, then employees are at risk of becoming dissatisfied and uncommitted. In such situations, employees usually attribute their unhappiness to their managers or to their organizations. They'll decide their organization has the wrong culture, for example. That kind of thinking often leads to a "migration cure" of leaving one organization for another, only to find similar dissatisfaction because the root of the career malaise has not been identified and addressed. One individual we consulted, a manager in the high-tech industry, went through three companies before realizing it wasn't the company he needed to change but his work. He had never wanted to be a manager but had agreed to a promotion because it offered more money and prestige. All he really wanted to do was design intricate machinery and mechanisms; he wanted to be an engineer again.

That story brings us to the second reason career development is handled poorly. The engineer was originally promoted to manager at the suggestion of the human resources department. Generally speaking, we have found that when career development is handed off to HR, problems arise. Many HR managers try to tackle career development using standardized tests such as the Myers-Briggs Type Indicator. There is nothing wrong with the Myers-Briggs and tests like it. In fact, they are excellent when used to help teams understand their own working dynamics. But personality type should not be the foundation of career development. Some HR managers do use the Strong Interest Inventory to get at life interests, which is better, but it suffers from being too general. The Strong helps people who want to know if they should be a Marine Corps sergeant or a ballet dancer, but it does little for people who say, "I know I want to work in business. Exactly what type of job is best for me?"

The bigger problem with allowing HR to handle career development is that it cuts the manager out of the process. Career development in general, and job sculpting in particular, requires an ongoing dialogue between an employee and his boss; it should not be shunted to another department, however good it may be. HR adds its value in training and supporting managers as career developers.

The Techniques of Job Sculpting

Job sculpting, then, begins when managers identify each employee's deeply embedded life interests. Sometimes an employee's life interest is glaringly obvious—she is excited doing one kind of work and dismal doing another. But much more often, a manager has to probe and observe.

Some managers worry that job sculpting requires them to play psychologist. They shouldn't worry. If they're good managers, they already play the role of psychologist intuitively. Managers *should* have a strong interest in the motivational psychology of their employees. In fact, they should openly express their willingness to help sculpt their employees' careers and to make the extra effort required to hold onto talented people.

Job sculpting, incidentally, can also be marketed externally to attract new hires. We have an unusual vantage point: we've seen close to a thousand new business professionals recruited and hired every year for the last 20 years. Without a doubt, the single most important thing on the minds of new MBAs is—not money!—but whether a position will move their long-term careers in a chosen direction. In fact, during a recent recruiting season, one employer—a Wall Street firm—gained a significant advantage over its competitors by emphasizing its commitment to career development. In both presentations and individual discussions, executives from the firm described its interest in and commitment to helping its professionals think about and manage their careers— a fact that many students cited as key to their choosing that firm.

If managers promise to job sculpt, of course they have to deliver. But how? Each change in assignment provides an opportunity to do some sculpting. For instance, a salesperson with an interest in *quantitative analysis* might be given new duties working with the marketing product manager and market research analysts—while remaining in sales. Or an engineer with an interest in *influence through language and ideas* might be given the task of helping the marketing communications people design sales support materials or user manuals—again, while retaining her primary role as an engineer.

But we have found that such intermittent patching attempts at job sculpting are not nearly as effective as bringing the process directly into the regular performance review. An effective performance review dedicates time to discussing past performance and plans for the future. In making job sculpting part of those conversations, it becomes systematized, and in becoming systematized, the chances of someone's career "falling through the cracks" are minimized.

Do managers need special training to job sculpt? No, but they do need to start listening more carefully when employees describe what they like and dislike about their jobs. Consider the case of a pharmaceutical company executive who managed 30 salespeople. In a performance review, one of her people offhandedly mentioned that her favorite part of the past year had been helping their division find new office space and negotiating for its lease. "That was a blast. I loved it," she told her boss. In the past, the executive would have paid the comment little heed. After all, what did it have to do with the woman's performance in sales? But listening with the ears of a job sculptor, the executive probed further, asking, "What made the search for new office space fun for you?" and "How was that different from what you do day-to-day?" The conversation revealed that the saleswoman was actually very dissatisfied and bored with her current position and was considering leaving. In fact, the saleswoman yearned for work that met her deeply embedded life interests, which had to do with *influence through language and ideas* and *creative production*. Her sales job encompassed the former, but it was only when she had the chance to think about the location, design, and layout of the new office that her creativity could be fully expressed. The manager helped the woman move to a position at company headquarters, where her primary responsibility was to design marketing and advertising materials.

Along with listening carefully and asking probing questions during the performance review, managers can ask employees to play an active role in job sculpting—before the meeting starts. In most corporate settings, the employee's preparation for a performance review includes a written assessment of accomplishments, goals for the upcoming review period, skill areas in need of development, and plans for accomplishing both goals and growth. During the review, this assessment is then compared to the supervisor's assessment.

But imagine what would happen if employees were also expected to write up their personal views of career satisfaction. Imagine if they were to prepare a few paragraphs on what kind of work they love or if they described their favorite activities on the job. Because so many people are unaware of their deeply embedded life interests—not to mention unaccustomed to discussing them with their managers—such exercises might not come easily at first. Yet they would be an excellent starting point for a discussion, ultimately allowing employees to speak more clearly about what they want from work, both in the short and long term. And that information would make even the best job-sculpting managers more effective.

Once managers and employees have discussed deeply embedded life interests, it's time to customize the next work assignment accordingly. In cases where the employee requires only a small change in his activities, that might just mean adding a new responsibility. For example, an engineer who has a deeply embedded life interest in *counseling and mentoring* might be asked to plan and manage the orientation of new hires. Or a logistics planner with a deeply embedded life interest in *influence through language and ideas* could be given the task of working on recruitment at college campuses. The goals here would be to give some immediate gratification through an immediate and real change in the job and to begin the process of moving the individual to a role that more fully satisfies him.

Sometimes, however, job sculpting calls for more sub-
stantial changes. Mark, the dissatisfied bank lending officer, is one example. Another is Carolyn, who was a star
industry analyst at a leading Wall Street firm. Carolyn
was so talented at designing and using sophisticated new
quantitative approaches to picking stocks that at one
point the head of the entire division remarked, "Carolyn
has brought our business into the twenty-first century."
That same year, she was ranked as the second most valuable person within the entire group—out of almost a
hundred very talented finance professionals. For the past
several years, senior managers had sought to ensure Carolyn's loyalty to the organization by awarding her generous raises and bonuses, making her one of their highest
paid people.

But Carolyn had one foot out the door. When she
received a huge raise (even by the standards of this firm
and her own compensation history), she was actually
angry, commenting to a friend, "That's typical of this
company; it thinks that it can solve every problem by
throwing money at it." Although she loved analysis and
mathematics, she had a strong desire to have a greater
impact on the decision making and direction of the
research group. She had definite opinions regarding what
kind of people they should be hiring, how the group
should be organized and the work assigned, and how the
group could most effectively work with other departments—in other words, she had deeply embedded life
interests in *enterprise control* and *managing people and
relationships.*

A performance review gave Carolyn a chance to
express her dreams and frustrations to her boss. Together they arrived at a "player-coach" role for Carolyn

as coordinator of research. She was still an analyst, but she also had taken on the responsibilities of guiding and directing several teams, making decisions about hiring and promotions, and helping set strategic direction. A year later, all parties agreed that the research group had never been more productive.

Job sculpting allowed Carolyn's firm to keep some of her extraordinary skills as an analyst while satisfying her desire to manage. But oftentimes job sculpting involves more sacrifice on the part of the organization. Remember that when Mark moved to his new job in business development, the bank lost a talented lending officer. Sometimes job sculpting requires short-term pain for long-term gain, although we would argue that in Mark's case—and in many others like it—they would have lost him soon enough anyway.

And one final caveat emptor. When job sculpting requires taking away parts of a job an employee dislikes, it also means finding someone new to take them on. If staffing levels are sufficient, that won't be a problem—an uninteresting part of one person's job may be perfect for someone else. At other times, however, there won't be a knight in shining armor to take on the "discarded" work. And at still other times, a manager may recognize that there is simply no way to accomplish the job sculpting the employee wants or even needs. (For instance, an engineering firm may not have activities to satisfy a person with a life interest in *influence through language and ideas*.) In such a case, a manager may have to make the hard choice to counsel a talented employee to leave the company.

Even with its challenges, job sculpting is worth the effort. In the knowledge economy, a company's most important asset is the energy and loyalty of its people—

the intellectual capital that, unlike machines and factories, can quit and go to work for your competition. And yet, many managers regularly undermine that commitment by allowing talented people to stay in jobs they're doing well at but aren't fundamentally interested in. That just doesn't make sense. To turbocharge retention, you must first know the hearts and minds of your employees and then undertake the tough and rewarding task of sculpting careers that bring joy to both.

It's a Matter of Degree

OVER THE PAST SEVERAL DECADES, countless studies have been conducted to discover what makes people happy at work. The research almost always focuses on three variables: ability, values, and life interests. In this article, we argue that life interests are paramount—but what of the other two? Don't they matter? The answer is yes, but less so.

Ability—meaning the skills, experience, and knowledge a person brings to the job—can make an employee feel competent. That's important; after all, research has shown that a feeling of incompetence hinders creativity, not to mention productivity. But although competence can certainly help a person get hired, its effect is generally short lived. People who are good at their jobs aren't necessarily engaged by them.

In the context of career satisfaction, values refer to the rewards people seek. Some people value money, others want intellectual challenge, and still others desire prestige or a comfortable lifestyle. People with the same abilities and life interests may pursue different careers based on their values. Take three people who excel at and love quantitative analysis. One might pursue a career as a professor of finance for the intellectual challenge. Another might go straight to Wall Street to reap the financial rewards. And a third might pursue whatever job track leads to the CEO's office—driven by a desire for power and influence.

Like ability, values matter. In fact, people rarely take jobs that don't match their values. A person who hates to travel would not jump at an offer from a management consulting firm. Someone who values financial security won't chase a career as an independent contractor. But people can be drawn into going down career paths because they have the ability and like the rewards—even though they're not interested in the work. After a short period of success, they become disenchanted, lose interest, and either quit or just work less productively.

That's why we have concluded that life interests are the most important of the three variables of career satisfaction. You can be good at a job—indeed, you generally need to be—and you can like the rewards you receive from it. But only life interests will keep most people happy and fulfilled over the long term. And that's the key to retention.

The Big Eight

WE HAVE FOUND THAT MOST people in business are motivated by between one and three deeply embedded life interests—long-held, emotionally driven passions for certain kinds of activities. Deeply embedded life interests are not hobbies or enthusiasms; they are innate passions that are intricately entwined with personality. Life interests don't determine what we're good at but what kinds of work we love.

Our conclusions about the number and importance of deeply embedded life interests have grown out of more than a decade of research into the drivers of career satisfaction. In 1986, we began interviewing professionals from a wide range of industries and functions as well as asking them to take a battery of psychological tests in order to assess what factors contributed to work satisfaction. Over the next dozen years, our database had grown to 650 people.

The results of our research were striking: scales on several of the tests we used clearly formed eight separate clusters. In other words, all business work could be broken down into eight types of core activities. By looking more closely at the content of the scales in each cluster and by cross-referencing this information to our interview data and counseling experience, we developed and tested a model of what we call "business core functions." These core functions represent the way deeply embedded life interests find expression in business. The following is a summary of each:

Application of Technology

Whether or not they are actually working as—or were trained to be—engineers, people with the life interest application of technology are intrigued by the inner workings of things. They are curious about finding better ways to use technology to solve business problems. We know a successful money manager who acts as his company's unofficial computer consultant because he loves the challenge of unlocking code. Indeed, he loves it more than his "day job"! People with the application-of-technology life interest often enjoy work that involves planning and analyzing production and operations systems and redesigning business processes.

It's often easy to recognize people with a strong application-of-technology life interest. They speak fondly of their college years when they majored in computer science or engineering. They read software magazines and manuals for fun. They comment excitedly when the company installs new hardware.

But sometimes the signs are more subtle. Application-of-technology people often approach business problems with a "let's take this apart and solve it" mind-set. And when introduced to a new process at work, they like to get under the hood and fully understand how it works rather than just turn the key and drive it. In a snapshot, application-of-technology people are the ones who want to know how a clock works because the technology excites them—as does the possibility that it could be tinkered with and perhaps improved.

Quantitative Analysis

Some people aren't just good at running the numbers, they excel at it. They see it as the best, and sometimes the only, way to figure out business solutions. Similarly, they see mathematical work as fun when others consider it drudgery, such as performing a cash-flow analysis, forecasting the future performance of an investment instrument, or figuring out the best debt/equity structure for a business. They might also enjoy building computer models in order to determine optimal production scheduling and to perform accounting procedures.

Not all "quant jocks" are in jobs that reflect this deeply embedded life interest. In fact, many of these individuals find themselves in other kinds of work because they have been told that following their true passion will narrow their career prospects. Yet these people are not difficult to miss, because regardless of their assignment, they gravitate toward numbers. Consider the HR professional who analyzes his organization by looking at compensation levels and benefits and by studying the ratio of managers to employees. Similarly, a marketing manager who loves analyzing customer research data—versus the subjective findings of focus groups—is probably a person with quantitative analysis at her core.

Theory Development and Conceptual Thinking

For some people, nothing brings more enjoyment than thinking and talking about abstract ideas. Think of Mark, the West Coast banker who was frustrated in his position because he did not have the opportunity to ponder big-picture strategy. Like Mark, people with this deeply embedded life interest are drawn to theory—the why of strategy interests them much more than the how. People with this interest can be excited by building business models that explain competition within a given industry or by analyzing the competitive position of a business within a particular market. Our research also shows that people with this deeply embedded interest are often drawn to academic careers. Some end up there; many do not.

How can you identify the people with this interest? For starters, they're not only conversant in the language of theory, but they also genuinely enjoy talking about abstract concepts. Often, these are the people who like thinking about situations from the "30,000 foot" level. Another clue: these individuals often subscribe to periodicals that have an academic bent.

Creative Production

Some people always enjoy the beginning of projects the most, when there are many unknowns and they can make something out of nothing. These individuals are frequently seen as imaginative, out-of-the-box thinkers. They seem most engaged when they are brainstorming or inventing unconventional solutions. Indeed, they seem to thrive on newness. The reason: creative production is one of their dominant deeply embedded life interests—making something original, be it a product or a process.

Our research shows that many entrepreneurs, R&D scientists, and engineers have this life interest. Many of them have an interest in the arts, but just as many don't. An entrepreneur we know has virtually no passion for the arts; his quite successful businesses over the years have included manufacturing decidedly unsexy paper bags and sealing tape.

There are, of course, many places in the business world where people with this interest can find satisfying work—new product development, for example, or advertising. Many people with this interest gravitate toward creative industries such as entertainment. Yet others, like one investment analyst we know, repress this life interest because they feel that it is "too soft" for business. Creative production, they believe, is for their off-hours.

Fortunately for managers, most creative-production people are not terribly hard to recognize. They wear their life interest on their sleeves—sometimes literally, by virtue of their choice of unconventional clothing, but almost always by how excited they are when talking about the new elements of a business or product. Oftentimes, they show little interest in things that are already established, no matter how profitable or state-of-the-art.

Counseling and Mentoring

For some people, nothing is more enjoyable than teaching—in business, that usually translates into coaching or mentoring. These individuals are driven by the deeply embedded life interest of counseling and mentoring, allowing them to guide employees, peers, and even clients to better performance. People with a high interest in counseling and mentoring are also often drawn to organizations, such as museums, schools, and hospitals, that provide products or services they perceive to hold a high social value. People like to counsel and mentor for many reasons. Some derive satisfaction when other people succeed; others love the feeling of being needed. Regardless, these people are drawn to work where they can help others grow and improve. We know, for instance, of a brand manager at a consumer goods company who was primarily responsible for designing her product's marketing and distribution plans. Yet she eagerly made time every week to meet one-on-one with several subordinates in order to provide feedback on their performance and answer any questions they had about the company and their careers. When it came time for her performance review, the brand manager's boss didn't bother to evaluate this counseling-and-mentoring work, saying that it wasn't technically part of the brand manager's job. It was, however, her favorite part.

People with a counseling-and-mentoring interest will make themselves known if their jobs include the opportunity to do so. But many people in this category don't get that chance. (New MBAs, in particular, are not asked to coach other employees for several years out.) However, you can sometimes identify counseling-and-mentoring people by their hobbies and volunteer work. Many are drawn to hands-on community service, such as the Big Brother Organization or literacy programs. People with a high interest in counseling and mentoring can be recognized by the fact that when they talk about their previous work they often talk fondly about the people who worked under them and where they are now—like a parent would talk about his or her children.

Managing People and Relationships

Longing to counsel and mentor people is one thing; wanting to manage them is another thing entirely. Individuals with this deeply embedded life interest enjoy dealing with people on a day-to-day basis. They derive a lot of satisfaction from workplace relationships—but they focus much more on outcomes than do people in the counseling-and-mentoring category. In other words, they're less interested in seeing people grow than in working with and through them to accomplish the goals of the business, whether it be building a product or making a sale. That is why people with this life interest often find happiness in line management positions or in sales careers.

Take Tom, a 32-year-old Harvard MBA who joined an Internet start-up in Silicon Valley—mainly because that was what all his classmates were doing. Tom had an undergraduate degree and work experience in engineering, and so his new company put him right to work in its technology division. Tom had no subordinates and no clients and mainly spent his days talking to other engineers and testing prototypes. It was the perfect job for someone with Tom's background, but not for someone with his life interest in managing people and relationships. After six months, he was miserable.

Tom was about to quit when the company announced it needed someone to help set up and run a new manufacturing plant in Texas. Tom pounced on the job—he would ultimately be leading a staff of 300 and negotiating frequently with suppliers. He got the job and still holds it today, five years later. His desire to motivate, organize, and direct people has been happily fulfilled.

Enterprise Control

Sarah, an attorney, is a person who has loved running things ever since she was a child. At age five, she set up her first lemonade stand and refused to let her older brother and sister help pour the juice, set prices, or collect money. (She did, however, let them flag down customers.) As a teenager, Sarah ran a summer camp in her backyard. And in college, she was the president of not one but three major groups, including the student government. People accuse her of being a control freak, and Sarah doesn't argue—she is happiest when she has ultimate decision-making authority. She feels great when she is in charge of making things happen.

Wanting too much control can be unhealthy, both for the people themselves and for their organizations, but some people are driven—in quite healthy ways—by a deeply embedded life interest in enterprise control. Whether or not they like managing people, these people find satisfaction in making the decisions that determine the direction taken by a work team, a business unit, a company division, or an entire organization. Sarah was not particularly happy as a lawyer—a career she pursued at the behest of an influential college instructor, and her mother, a lawyer herself. But she did eventually fulfill her life interest in enterprise control when, after coming back from maternity leave, she asked to run the company's New York office, with 600 attorneys, clerks, and other staff. It was, she says, "a match made in heaven."

Enterprise-control people are easy to spot in organizations. They seem happiest when running projects or teams; they enjoy "owning" a transaction such as a trade or a sale. These individuals also tend to ask for as much responsibility as possible in any work situation. Pure interest in enterprise control can be seen as an interest in deal making or in strategy—a person with this life interest wants to be the CEO, not the COO. Investment bankers, for example, don't run ongoing operations but often demonstrate a very strong interest in enterprise control.

Influence Through Language and Ideas

Some people love ideas for their own sake, but others love expressing them for the sheer enjoyment that comes from storytelling, negotiating, or persuading. Such are people with the deeply embedded life interest of influence through language and ideas. They feel most fulfilled when they are writing or speaking—or both. Just let them communicate.

People in this category sometimes feel drawn to careers in public relations or advertising, but they often find themselves elsewhere, because speaking and writing are largely considered skills, not careers. And yet for some, effective communication is more than just a skill—it's a passion. One way to identify these individuals in your organization is to notice who volunteers for writing assignments. One MBA student we counseled joined a large consulting firm where, for three years, she did the standard analytical work of studying industry dynamics and so forth. When she heard that a partner had to create a report for a new client "that liked to see things in writing," she quickly offered her services. Her report was so persuasive—and she had such a fun experience writing it—that she was soon writing for the company full-time. Had her deeply embedded interest in communication not been met in-house, she surely would have sought it elsewhere.

People with strong interests in influence through language and ideas love persuasion of all sorts, spoken and written, verbal and visual. They enjoy thinking about their audience (whether one person or millions) and the best way to address them. And they enjoy spending time on communications both outside and inside the company. One woman we know who is the head of strategic planning for an entertainment company says, "I spend at least 75% of my time thinking about how to sell our findings to the CEO and other members of the executive team." Clearly, the amount of mental energy this executive devotes to persuasion characterizes her as an influence-through-language-and-ideas person.

As we've noted, it is not uncommon for managers to sense that an employee has more than one deeply embedded life interest. That is possible. The pairs of life interests that are most commonly found together are listed below:

Enterprise Control with Managing People and Relationships. These individuals want to run a business on a day-to-day basis but are also challenged by—and enjoy—managing people.

Managing People and Relationships with Counseling and Mentoring. These are the ultimate people-oriented professionals. They have a strong preference for service-management roles, enjoying the frontline aspects of working in high customer-contact environments. They also tend to enjoy human resources management roles.

Quantitative Analysis with Managing People and Relationships. These individuals like finance and finance-related jobs, yet they also find a lot of pleasure managing people toward goals.

Enterprise Control with *Influence Through Language and Ideas.* This is the most common profile of people who enjoy sales. (An interest in Managing People and Relationships is also often high among satisfied salespeople.) This combination is also found extensively among general managers—especially those who are charismatic leaders.

Application of Technology with *Managing People and Relationships.* This is the engineer, computer scientist, or other technically oriented individual who enjoys leading a team.

Creative Production with *Enterprise Control.* This is the most common combination among entrepreneurs. These people want to start things and dictate where projects will go. "Give me the ball and I'll score" is their mantra.

Originally published in September–October 1999
Reprint 99502

About the Contributors

TIMOTHY BUTLER is Director of M.B.A. Career Development Programs at the Harvard Business School, where he has worked since 1984. He was formerly on the faculty of the psychology department at the State University of New York in Albany. Together with Dr. James Waldroop, he developed the Internet-based interactive career assessment program *Career-Leader*. His work focuses on executive coaching and career development assessment and counseling. He has worked with a wide range of organizations in both the manufacturing and service sectors, from *Fortune* 50 corporations to smaller high-growth firms. He has coauthored several books and articles including *Maximum Success: Changing the 12 Behavior Patterns that Keep You From Getting Ahead*, *Discovering Your Career in Business*, "The Executive as Coach" (*Harvard Business Review*), "Finding the Job You *Should* Want" (*Fortune*), and "Eight Failings That Bedevil the Best" (*Fortune*).

PETER CAPPELLI is the George W. Taylor Professor of Management at the Wharton School of the University of Pennsylvania. He is also Director for the Center for Human Resources and serves as a Research Associate at the National Bureau of Economic Research. His latest book is *The New Deal at Work: Managing the Market-Driven Workforce*.

BETSY A. COLLARD is Director of the Office of Volunteer Relations at Stanford University. Ms. Collard has spent most of her professional life in the area of career development, and is nationally recognized for her leadership in this field. For twenty years she served as Director of Programs and Innovation at the Career Action Center, where she was responsible for the growth of career development programs and services for *Fortune* 500 companies. She is the author of *The High-Tech Career Book* and the coauthor of "Beyond Balance to Life Quality: The Integration of Work and Life."

DIANE COUTU is Senior Editor at the *Harvard Business Review*, where she specializes in issues of organization and psychology. Before joining *HBR*, she worked as a communications specialist for McKinsey & Company; prior to that she was a foreign correspondent for *Time* and *The Wall Street Journal, Europe*. Ms. Coutu studied literature at Yale University and politics, philosophy, and economics at Oxford University, where she was a Rhodes Scholar. She has been an Affiliate Scholar at the Boston Psychoanalytic Society and Institute and was BPSI's 1998 Silberger Scholar.

CLAUDIO FERNÁNDEZ-ARÁOZ is a Partner at Egon Zehnder International and a member of its Executive Committee, as well as the leader of internal professional development for the firm's 56 offices worldwide. He is also the Manager of the Buenos Aires office. Before joining Egon Zehnder International, Mr. Fernández-Aráoz worked as an Engagement Manager for McKinsey & Company in Spain and Italy. Since 1986, he has spent most of his time working on senior executive search assignments while conducting research on the relevance of emotional intelligence and the differentiating competencies for top leadership and managerial positions.

HERMINIA IBARRA is Professor of Organizational Behavior at the Harvard Business School. A member of the HBS faculty since 1989, Professor Ibarra investigates what makes people successful in their careers. Her research in this area encompasses a range of topics including career transitions, social networks, professional identity, and women's careers. Her articles on these topics have appeared in leading management journals including *Administrative Science Quarterly, Academy of Management Journal, Academy of Management Review,* and *Social Psychology Quarterly.* Before joining Harvard Business School, Professor Ibarra was Teaching Fellow at the Yale School of Organization and Management, prior to which she worked on innovation research at the Universite Libre in Brussels, Belgium. She is currently working on a book about how and why people make major career changes at mid-career.

JAMES WALDROOP, the Principal and Cofounder of Peregrine Partners, is Associate Director of M.B.A. Career Development Programs at the Harvard Business School, where he has worked since 1981. Together with Dr. Timothy Butler, he developed the Internet-based interactive career assessment program *CareerLeader* (www.careerdiscovery.com). *CareerLeader* is currently used by over 100 M.B.A. programs and corporations around the world and includes the *Business Career Interest Inventory,* the *Management and Professional Reward Profile,* and the *Management and Professional Abilities Profile,* all instruments designed by Waldroop and Butler. He has coauthored *Maximum Success: Changing the 12 Behavior Patterns that Keep You From Getting Ahead, Discovering Your Career in Business,* "The Executive as Coach" (*Harvard Business Review*), "Finding the Job You *Should* Want" (*Fortune*), and "Eight Failings That Bedevil the Best" (*Fortune*). In addition to his writing, he is a regular contributor to CNBC, a Diplomate in Counseling Psychology, and a Fellow of the Massachusetts Psychological Association.

ROBERT H. WATERMAN, JR. is the coauthor of *In Search of Excellence.* Since that book's publication in 1982, he has written three other books: *The Renewal Factor, Adhocracy: The Power to Change*, and *What America Does Right*. He is Founding Director of the AES Corporation, now the world's largest independent power producer, and serves on the board of several for-profit and nonprofit organizations including eProNet, the Restless Leg Syndrome Foundation, the World Wildlife Fund, and the Center for Excellence in Nonprofits. Outside his business role, Mr. Waterman paints in watercolor and oil; his last gallery show was in March 2000. Prior to his work as an author, director, and artist, Mr. Waterman spent 21 years at McKinsey & Company, serving in or managing offices in San Francisco, Japan, and Australia.

JUDITH A. WATERMAN is Founder and Chief Executive Officer of Career Management Group and Founding Director of eProNet, the exclusive web-based job search, placement, and career management service for alumni of 20 of the top colleges and universities in the United States. In her counseling practice, she works with individuals to promote both their professional and personal development, and in her organizational consulting, she emphasizes solutions beneficial to both the individual and the company. An avid supporter of sustainable development, she currently serves on the Marine Leadership Committee for the World Wildlife Fund. She has also served as Chair of the Advisory Board for the College of Music at the University of Colorado and as a member of their Entrepreneurship Center for Music Industry Advisory Council. Ms. Waterman is the author of several computer programs as well as many publications.

SUZY WETLAUFER is the Editor of the *Harvard Business Review*.

Index